TAUNTON REFERENCE LIBRARY
PAUL STREET
TAUNTON
TA1 3XZ

REFERENCE LIBRARY

FOR USE IN LIBRARY ONLY

000
.752

This book must be returned or renewed by the latest date above or at the next visit of the mobile library. Normally books may be renewed if not in demand.

ARCADIA

Slot Machines
of
Europe and America

ARCADIA

Slot Machines of Europe and America

Jean-Claude Baudot

Costello

Published in English in 1988

First published in French in 1983 - Credit Communal de Belgique

© Jean-Claude Baudot

All rights reserved

All enquiries to D J Costello (Publishers) Ltd
43 High Street Tunbridge Wells Kent TN1 1XL

Baudot, Jean-Claude, *1933–*
   Arcadia: slot machines of Europe and
  America.
  1. Coin slot recreational machines,
  ca 1850–ca 1950
  I. Title   II. Machines a sous. *English*
  688.7

   ISBN 0–7104–2052–8
Typeset by texTech
Tunstall House Mountfield East Sussex TN32 5LB

Printed and bound in Great Britain by
Purnell Book Production Ltd
Paulton Bristol BS18 5LQ

Photography by Gérard Pestarque IED France
56 rue d'Aguesseau 92100 Boulogne France

Translated from the French by Anthony Carter

CONTENTS

Introduction	7
Early History of Automatic Games	13
Prohibition	19
Art and the Slot Machines	22
Methods of Classification	24
Musical Slot Machines	26
Wall Machines	31
Special Slot Machines	41
Drop Case Machines	55
Roulettes	62
Shooting Machines	74
3 Reel Machines	78
Trade Stimulators	97
Scales and Strength Machines	108
Electric Shock Machines and Viewers	114
Fortune Tellers	120
Vending Machines	123
Pintables, Billiards and Bagatelle	132
Juke Boxes	135
Other Illustrations	137
Identification	155
French Manufacturers	157
Bibliography	161
Index of Machines	163

Introduction

In the first days of Babylon, if one is to believe the Borgias, barbers used to sell rectangles of bone or parchment, decorated with symbols, for copper coins. By daylight a draw was held and the winners received silver coins. The game was simple and the question was how this rudimentary lottery could be made more exciting. The Borgias' answer, disturbing as it might seem, was to increase the bets excessively, gambling one's loves, one's whole future, even one's life.

The slot machine of our Babylon is quite different, relying purely upon the technical to whet the gambler's appetite. Luck is not always involved in deciding the winner and slot machines are far from being total games of chance, some can be hardly said to be games as opposed to the Babylonian lottery excesses.

This doubtless accounts for the frequent repression of, and feeling against the machines. Despite the profits made from slot machines, public authorities look upon them with deep suspicion. That is when they are not, as in the times of prohibition, smashing them. Traditionalists show a blind prejudice and intellectuals, even those most involved in social trends, generally see the machine as beneath their dignity. A good example of the latter is that of Huizinga. In his *Homo Ludens* an imposing study of the role of gambling in cultures, there is not a mention of these machines which were increasing in importance beneath his very nose! Roger Caillois was one of the first sociologists to take slot machines into account. Wearing his moralist's hat he condemned them out of hand as being 'pointless and worthless games', pseudo games, which only 'replace the boredom by a routine disguised as entertainment'. For him the slot-machine attracted the same anathema as the pinball machine.

The fact remains, however, that slot machines have made their mark on half of the globe, and for nearly a century now, hordes of players have been seduced either by the unpredictable shining ball or by the transformation of a single coin into a veritable shower of gold.

Certain American states have even put them into their own special 'reservations'; casinos, hotels and amusement centres. Here the one-armed bandits 'hold-up' rich and poor alike, many of whom are housewives spending what they have managed to save from their housekeeping money. In Japan long lines of the young, the old, students and functionaries alike take a noisy and mysterious pleasure in feeding the voracious mouths. In Europe, things are not perhaps taken to quite the same extreme. In Italy (despite being the birthplace of the lottery) and in France their use has been carefully and scrupulously controlled. But by 1930 the British were already feeding their machines millions of pennies a year, to the great benefit of the owners and the manufacturers. Thus the passion for playing and the bait of winning led to an incredible increase in the numbers of these machines and at the same time attracted a thinly veiled general disapproval. The more their economic value grows, the more their cultural standing approaches zero; but is that any reason to write them off? Collector Jean-Claude Baudot's answer is to exhibit the machines in a museum, out of their natural habitat, so that they can been seen in a fresh light.

The observer is struck immediately by the huge variety and range of slot-machines: giant, dwarf, skinny, pot-bellied, grotesque, square, wooden, cast in iron or brass, chrome plated, some gross and beast-like, others decorated with primitive designs or geometric figures. The smartest are in Art Nouveau style, the trickiest decorated with horns of plenty and this same diversity is reflected in their functions. The twin elements of financial gain (money corrupts) and just playing for pleasure are present to varying degrees. Some machines are more like vending machines than amusement machines, simply supplying cigarettes, chocolate and post-cards. About the only element of pleasure one gets from taking the egg shaped sweet from the hen's behind or a piece of chewing gum from an elephant's trunk, is that you've bought it without any other human involvement! Here money is more important than playing. But the majority of machines are less blatant, selling only the right to play and eventual reward - straightaway fed back into the machine for another game. To put a coin into a slot is to introduce a little bit of uncertainty into one's life. 'Shall I manage to get the ball in the hole? Shall I get the horoscope I want? Shall I manage to line up the two cherries with the lemon and hit the jackpot?'

How can one possibly classify these machines? Should it be according to the player's skill and luck, his concentration and co-ordination at a peak, falling away to a mindless stare at a multi-coloured disc? Should it be according to the amount of energy (mechanical, electrical or electro mechanical) set off by the player himself? Or should they be classified according to the extent to which they are corruptions of existing games like poker, liar dice or billiards, or even by how original they are? There's also a case for classification by the pay-out. In this context it is worth remembering that one-armed bandits, with twenty symbols on each of the three reels, have no fewer than 8,000 combinations, only 12 of which pay out.

The slot-machine is not only the most ubiquitous of all nineteenth century technical artefacts, bequeathed to the western world, it is also the most ambiguous. Can it truly be called a machine? Of course it can, since it has movement: of course it cannot since the movement produces nothing useful. On one hand, with its levers, pulleys, gears, sliding axles and camshafts, everything points to mechanical power. When a spring is released to propel a ball up a slope, whenever a lever causes a reaction in a rotation, when a coin falls and causes a disc to turn, the slot machine, like any other machine, is exciting and controlling natural forces. In a complex and often ingenious way the slot machine combines in one several of the machines described by Heron of Alexandria, twenty centuries ago. But the composite machine lacks the integrity of pure mechanics: physical power does no work; if a wheel turns at all, it's the Wheel of Fortune, and any movement is part of a game. Whether rotational or vertical any transmission of movement culminates in complete unproductivity: within minutes or seconds, the ball goes back to where it started, the drum stops turning, the coin is safely in the box and that is it!

As far as mechanism is concerned, the slot-machine appears to be an anti-motor. As far as economics, it is anti-productive. It wastes any effort and investment put into it. Give it something and it will do nothing with it, using all its technical resources to achieve nothing.

It is true that all games promise no more than a means of spending time, skill and money: they are all strictly unproductive, never paying out more than has been fed in. They are all based on a negation of work, and it is particularly ironic that in its social context the slot-machine has reversed its capitalistic and industrial role, thereby consuming rather than producing wealth. It is clear that such a paradoxical instrument could be found only in a mechanically-orientated world, both as a by-product and a counter product of mechanics. Machines renewed interest in gambling and gambling took over the machines. Not only were machines made more pleasurable, but their image changed considerably. If the 18th Century was the age of the game then the 19th Century brought us into the era of the mechanical game.

At the end of the last century and at the beginning of this one, a number of writers and artists devoted themselves to social relationships or even the logic of sexual relationships in terms of machinery, the machine being attributed with a regulatory role in society. In his essay *Les Machines Celibataires* Michel Carrouges made a study of such people whose attitudes were also to be the object of an ambitious study by Harald Szeemann. Both works clearly analysed Kafka, de Roussel, de Duchamp and Jules Verne on this, as well as examining Freud's *Appareil Psychique*, and Villiers de l'Isle d'Adam's *Etres-electro - humains* with reference to the modern trend of seeing the machine as the origin of Man. The modest slot-machine can hardly equate with Carrouge's thesis, but it unites player and machine into one entity, one dependent upon the other, and it also plays a part in the interplay of mechanics, eroticism and religion. Eroticism is suggested by the slit into which coins are slipped and psychoanalysts certainly see anal connotations, just as they see phallic symbolism in the pinball machine. The cruciform shapes on some machines and the mysteries of numbers lead to religious connotation.

So with a mixture of interest and maybe some disquiet, we learn that a slot-machine is not just a simple device for turning wheels or propelling balls, but an extension of man as man is an extension of the machine. What is more they assume human traits like the greedy mouth, the pot belly and the sphincter from which spills a diarrhoea of coins. Perhaps the machines are more like the anthropoids admired so much by men: so like man, but not quite man and thus enigmatic. How should we take them - Would you like to play with me? as the Martian said to the slot machine in the casino, thus putting the status of the machine in perspective. Not quite a human, but more than just a fool, the robot is a partner with a difference. Inversely, in line with the laws of play, the more humanised the machine becomes the more the player becomes a machine.

Watching Americans playing the one-armed bandits and Japanese the *pachinko* makes one think of factory workers on the line: machines rather than humans, robots no longer needing to think or reason. Caillois sums it up like this, 'The absurdity of the whole thing robs the act of any intelligent attribute: it is never ending, producing nothing but a result.' The Greek word *mekhane* equally means a trick, a ruse or a machine. Slot-machines are definitely more full of tricks than one would imagine.

For those who cannot come to terms with these machines, but who are fascinated by them, the only solution is to see them as toys, not games. Collect them like Jean-Claude Baudot, photograph them like Gérard Pestarque, or quite simply dream about them.

Yves Hersant
Sociologist

The Early History of Automatic Games

1

In 200 BC Heron of Alexandria in his book *Pneumatic* clearly and precisely describes the form and the mechanism of the first known automatic vending machine. It delivered holy water, blessed by the priests and was in the shape of an ancient vase with a slit in the top of the cover big enough to take a five - drachma coin. As the coin dropped upon a lever, it delivered a drop of holy water from a watertight container inside the vase. With this business acumen the priests were but a step away from the slot machine as we know it.

There are no more recorded developments until the year 1449 when an unknown genius built the oldest known automatic ball game. It resembled a little wooden wardrobe about 80cm high with a metal spring at the bottom which threw three ivory balls upwards to some sculptured figurines. Each time the spring was released, the figurines put out their right hand. To win, the player had to send the greatest number of balls into the outstretched hands. No money was involved but it was truly an automatic game thanks to the spring which made the balls move. This game, its case riddled with woodworm, is in Spain at the Grupo Invenciones du Museo Teenico de Barcelona.

Painter, sculptor, engineer, architect and scholar, Leonardo da Vinci was bound to have been interested in automation, but so many inventions are attributed to him that we cannot be sure of the extent of his contribution. What we do know is that at that period in Rome, like Leonardo, the politician Nicolo Padroni was an extraordinary organiser of festivals and displays. It would have been unusual if the two men had not met and Nicolo asked Leonardo to create some new amusements for him. The great artist designed several projects some of which must surely have come to fruition. We do know that Roman guests did play on an authentic mechanical billiard table whose remains can be found at the Museo Antico, Milan.

In 1702 in Petersburg, Tchimurowski built a billiards game with automatic holes which was exceptionally precise mathematically.

46 years later at Konigsberg in Germany, Johan Ferdinand Clebsch, mathematician and progenitor of a long line of famous mathematicians, invented and built a spectacular and extremely complex automatic puppet game. This game has disappeared without trace but the instructions for use are in the hands of Count Blenheim's family at Pochlarm, Lower Austria. The game was for two players. Each had to insert a florin to set four dolls moving on one side and three on the other - all seven suspended by strings allowing them to dance on a board. As they danced, they collided. The game was to knock your opponent's doll down a hole. Whoever managed to keep his three dolls standing won the other player's florin.

1 Coin Operated Holy water machine described by Heron of Alexandria (about 200BC).

The eighteenth century also saw the growth of automatic snuff boxes in English taverns. The customer slid a half-penny into the slot and pressed a button. The lid opened and he was able to take one pinch of snuff and no more than a pinch! As the quantity taken depended upon the honesty of the customer, the boxes became known as Honour Boxes, typifying the well known English sense of fair play! However, even if the money element was present, this was neither a game nor an automatic gambling machine. At the most it was the very first automatic snuff vending machine.

On the other hand, at this time in Germany, ingenious lights games machines were being manufactured. Several players could take part and by presing a spring each of them set off as many fire works as he could. The spaces where these light effects appeared were numbered and each player put his money on a certain number. So the principle of roulette existed over two hundred years ago.

In 1818 from Smyrna came the perfume vending machine, the invention of Armenian, Narodiow. Four years later English bookseller, Richard Carlisle, came up with the idea of a machine to sell banned books, banking on the machine's anonymity to protect him from prosecution: a slight miscalculation since he was prosecuted.

The first coin operated slot machine in the United States was the Penny Papers based on an old English patent, built in 1839 to sell cigarette papers: exceptionally it was protected by law.

In the Orient, great interest was shown in automatic games, and in 1850 at Peking, by command of Chinses Emperor Tao-Kwang-Hwang-Ti, an exhibition of dolls and games was organised. In Europe, as in Asia, circus performers often carried with them a magic machine which was the basis, if not the whole content, of their act. Sometimes these machines were automatic ones, which is why the 1850 exhibition was able to show more than 400 Chinese automatic games representing six centuries of evolution. Sixteen years later, the same exhibition was mounted at the Imperial National Museum, Peking. The machines still worked so well that, on payment, visitors were allowed to play them. In nine months this special levy brought the Emperor a jackpot of 142,000 gold tals from 45,000 playing visitors.

Rudolph Friedrich Alfred Clebsch (Johann's grandson) invented a mathematical ball game. Each game lasted three minutes, a bell ringing at the start and the end. This game was recently exhibited in the Heimat Museum at Konigsberg.

In 1857 an English patent was taken out for an automatic postage stamp machine, and ten years later a German inventor built similar machines selling such articles as cigarettes and handkerchiefs.

Towards the midddle of the century interest in automatic vending machines also developed in France and various other countries.

The first animated cast-iron money box, made by John Hall, appeared in the USA in 1871. Another American, William H Fruen, patented a drinks machine on 28th January 1884 and in 1888 Thomas Adams, the leading chewing gum distributor, introduced his machine, the Adams New York Chewing Gum, to the American market on a grand scale.
So the end of the century brought the birth of the automatic machine as we know it today, with lots of patents and small run productions. There are few surviving machines from this period thanks to Prohibition, among other things. There are two special dates to note: in 1891 Edison commercialised automatic operated phonographs and in 1892, Emmanuel Perlebach introduced multi- coloured lights into an improved version of Clebsch's game.

With the exception then of the priests of Ancient Egypt it was Emperors and Kings who ordered automats and automatic games from scientific and ingenious craftsmen. Again very few remain for they were unique models.

Then followed the rich and the showmen, so fascinated was man by automatic games but it was only at the end of the nineteenth century that mass production of machines began.

A multitude of engineers, some qualified, some self-taught, often geniuses, invented machines for all purposes. De Dion, Krieger, Renault, Mercedes made their name in the car industry for example, whilst Fey, Clawson, Bussoz, Mills, Caille, Watling, Loubet, Nau and Jennings left their mark on automatic machines.

2

3

4

5

7

6

2 & 3   Interiors in Paris bistros. Notice the roulette type of slot machine and two wall mounted ball games.

4   Target practice

5   Fernandel playing a Bussoz roulette machine (Marcade collection)

6   Interior of Bistro with two wall mounted ball machines

7   Parisian kiosk of the Belle Epoque

Prohibition

The poor old slot machine was certainly born at an inauspicious time. Even before conception most countries had a complex web of regulations controlling playing for money.

In France on 1st March 1781, Louis XVI had made a royal proclamation at Versailles on forbidden games, confirming all edicts and decrees against games of chance made by his royal predecessors. In addition to this, he banned any game which did not provide an equal chance of winning. In Year II, in the name of the Republic, the Convention decreed the suspension of all lotteries, and applied the Penal Code, articles 410, 475 and 477 to games of chance.

In France the professional automatic industry began in the 1890s. In 1902 the Paris Prefecture published a circular only permitting machines to distribute 20 and 30 centime drinks tokens, thus directly banning any machine giving out money. On 19th July 1906 a circular from the Ministry of Justice extended the ban to machines giving food and drink tokens. This was repealed two months later in a new circular of 29th September. Already inconsistencies were creeping in.

It was French president Georges Clemenceau who saved the automatic machine with his circular of June 22nd 1909. 'The only machines allowed are those which pay out tokens interchangeable against a single drink worth no more than 30 centimes which must be consumed in the same premises where the machine is in use. The game must be played by placing a coin, and no longer a token, into the slot'. Clear and simple - and a handy means of raising revenue! From 1910, each machine was taxed at 10F per annum, far from the 5,000 new Francs of Maury's 1982 government! However this tax did bring in 1,200,000 gold francs, telling us that in 1911 there were 120,000 machines officially in use.

Clemenceau's successors at the Ministry of the Interior were to introduce such an avalanche of amendments that they made the situation more obscure. The worried bar owners once again faced the threat of total prohibition as they found ways around the laws. They refer only to 'sweet venders', a nice euphemism for the banned jackpots alongside which were placed vending attachments selling rolls of mints.

In face of such abuse of the law, the axe finally fell on August 31st 1937, with the total prohibition of slot machines of any kind. The move was in fact just one facet of an international wave of anti gambling legislation which saw the outright banning of coin freed gambling games in all the major western nations.

In France, the situation has remained wonderfully paradoxical. Slot machines have been banned since 1937, their importation allowed since 1973 and taxed since 1982. The Devil looks after his own!

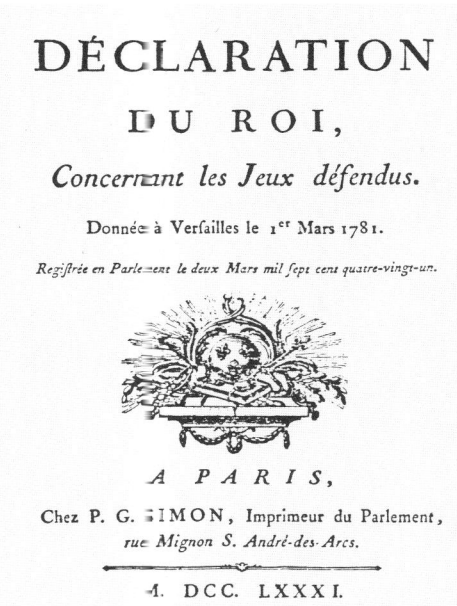

8 Louis XVI decree concerning banned games.

These are some of the laws and regulations that were passed :

In France - Statute of 1st July 1781

Decrees of The First Republic in the second and third months of the second year

Articles 410, 475, 477 of the penal code

Law of 21st May 1836 modified by the law of 18th July 1924

Circulars of August 1902, 25th December 1905, 19th July 1906, 27th September 1906, 22nd September 1909

Article 62 of the Finance Law of 1910

Circulars in 1919 and 22nd November 1927, 1st February 1930, 6th February 1931, 4th April 1934, 8th April 1935, 26th December 1935, 17th April 1936, 17th November 1936, 31st August 1937

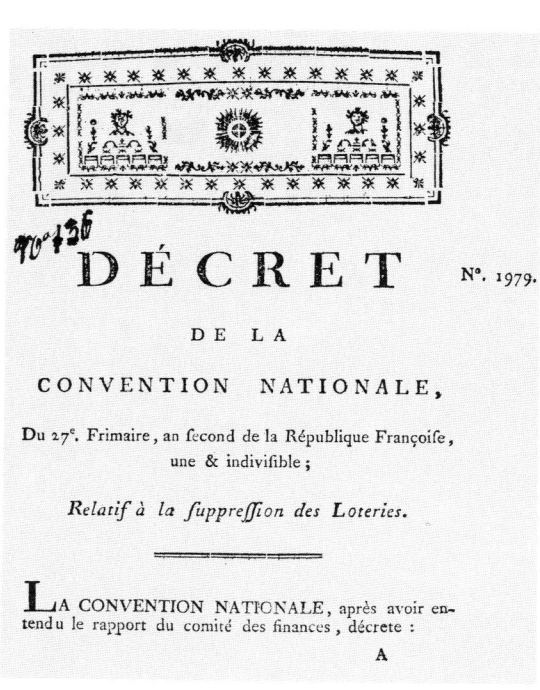

9 National Convention decree abolishing lotteries

10 Notice banning slot machines (law of 27th December 1914)

Customs Order no 2751 of 15/16th February 1973 and circular of December 1974

In Germany - Statute 33 of 22nd May 1935 banning coin freed gambling games

In USA - Johnson Act of 1951 setting the Federal seal upon the total prohibition of all coin freed gambling games

In UK - Betting and Gaming Act 1960 legalising the use of coin freed games of chance : a milestone in automatics history

Art and the Slot Machine

*Irresistible games of chance, seductive
flashing slot machines, some over a hundred years old,
are valued for what they are - astonishing
small works of popular art.*

Just as motor car manufacturers in their hundreds turned out lots of short run vehicles at the beginning of the century, so dozens of craftsmen devoted their creative talents to the slot machine.

The sculpted wooden boxes have beautifully worked front panels depicting flowers, animals, personalities and cafe life, hunting and sporting scenes. They were hand painted, printed or chromolithographed and fixed onto a bright velvet backing.

Weekend amateurs applied their boundless ingenuity to what lay behind the decoration - the mechanical side of things. Their task was easy when it was just a matter of recirculating balls which dropped into a cup, but rather more complex when the drum had to stop at a different spot each time.

A slot machine is popular art at its finest. Many manufacturers were influenced whether consciously or not by contemporary trends in art. A Napoleon III weighing machine (fig 129) is recognisable by its baroque mouldings typical of the era. Machines with evocative names from classical art are not uncommon - *The Sphinx* (fig 51), *Iris* (fig 62), *Fire* (fig 137), *The Egyptian* (fig 143). Sometimes slot machines were themselves an art form. *Puck* (fig 1). *Frog Pond* (fig 28), *The Smile* (fig 24), *Bussoz's roulette* (fig 58), *The Electra* shooting game (fig 80), the post-card machine (fig 150), belong to Art Nouveau, just as others belong to Art Deco: *Liberty Commercial* (fig 30), *Password* (fig 37), *The Derby* (fig 71), *Lightning* (fig 77), *Blue War Eagle* (fig 104), *Dough Boy* (fig 103), *Vapolux* (fig 154), *The Cyclone* (fig 151), *The Petrol Pump* (fig 157). As for *The Boxomat* (fig 33) it can be said that the structure of the box was clearly influenced by the cubism of a Goerg or a Picasso.

Nor is it surprising that there are several exceptional examples of primitive art represented with machines like *The Future* (fig 6), *The Clowns* (fig 10) and *Old Man Bidard* (fig 29).

If we accept Mark Twain's comment 'Everybody knew that it was possible except those who didn't know!', the builders, engineers and inventors of automatic machines of the Belle Epoque were unstoppable innocents. This naivety is easy to see in the way they decorated their work, fine examples of primitive art in moulded cast iron or painted metal. *Pierrot* (fig 9) has to send a ball into the sun, *The Matador* (fig 42) fights in the ring to the applause of the crowd. The hunters in *The Elk* (fig 43) putting up their tent, *The Negro Ball* (fig 123) laughs, *Uncle Sam* (fig 134) has a solemn smile and the *Electrified Pig* (fig 139) looks great with his four leaf clover in lieu of a bow-tie.

Some signed their work, others through fear of prosecution or forgetfulness did not. But with slot machines, as sculpture, it is not the signature that makes the artist, it is the piece of work itself.

Methods of Classification

When one is interested in automatic money machines, all classifications are possible: chronological, by manufacturer, by type or name of machine. The first two pose problems because one can not always identify the manufacturer or be sure about the exact date of manufacture. The chapter on identification and sources of information at the end of the book discusses this further. There is an alphabetical index with the name of each machine plus the page number. This groups them in their most obvious classification by type or family of machine. Despite this some models could fit in two different categories - a musical roulette machine could well be found under musical slot machines. No system is perfect however and it is not always easy to be objective.

163 machines are illustrated in the main body of the book with identifying numbers corresponding to the text. The unnumbered references, set in smaller type, refer to a further 96 machines. All these are illustrated in the last section of the book.

The dimensions are shown as height x width x depth

The year shown is that in which the model was created.

The Machines

Musical Slot Machines

Musical slot machines are to automatic machines what the Rolls-Royce is to the motor-car: majestic, proud, a little behind the times, but tried and tested. The music-box became a ruse to distract the attention of the authorities, following the draconian regulations of the end of the last century and the early twentieth century in certain areas of the USA. The result was semi-prohibition. However, manufacturers, ever far sighted and ready to adapt to the current rulings, offered their expensive prestige models in two versions: with or without a music-box. In difficult times these music-boxes served as an alibi: the instruction plate, with great candour, stated that this was an amusement machine built specifically for the playing of music and that any money won had to be played again until it had all gone. As it was totally impossible to catch anybody flouting the law, the authorities were powerless.

THE OWL
USA, Mills 1897 (158x68x42cm). Mills had great commercial success with this sturdy and cheap model. It is the best known of the big musical slot-machines. Through the years a dozen variations have been introduced. (p 138 fig B)

THE OWL
USA, Mills 1897 (158x68x42cm). The majority of the big American floor machines were sold with the option of an incorporated music-box or not as desired. (p 138 fig D)

1 THE PUCK
USA, Caille 1900 (168x65x42cm). The mechanism is based upon the roulette system. Having put just one, or several, coins in the slots correspondiong to the chosen colours, the player pulls down the lever on the right side facing him. The disc begins to turn on its axis for up to ten seconds, the length of a tune, then the semi-circular marker at the top of the disc is lowered, stopping the disc instantly. If the player is in luck, the machine automatically pays out the winnings (from 2 to 20 times the coin's value) which drop into the hole above the music.

1

2 THE PERFECTION
USA, Caille circa 1900 (152x55x40). This is the second model manufactured by Arthur Caille before 1900, just after *The Reliable*. It is interesting to remember that Arthur created The Caille Co in 1897 and his brother Adolf, The Caille-Scheimer Co in 1900, then the two brothers went on in 1901 to merge their companies under the famous name The Caille Brothers Company.

3 L'ORACLE
USA, Caille circa 1910 (159x63x42cm). Only the decoration on the polychromatic metal dial changes. The Oracle is certainly a variation of Caille's original *Lion*, which was better known at the time but now is very rare.

4 THE MUSICAL FLOOR MACHINE
USA, Caille circa 1900 (144x50x36cm). The name has been coined only because the model does not appear in any catalogue and this machine seems to be the sole known example. The music box is hidden.

5 THE RELIABLE
USA, Caille circa 1897 (144x50x36cm). This model, hardly known in the States, was however manufactured according to the plate by The Caille Company, Toledo, Ohio. The mechanism is in bronze, but is very simple when compared to the big Cailles built later. The box is narrow. It could be that this firm was trying to rival the *Owl* of Mills and, when the attempt failed, the unsold stock was sent to Europe where Caille had an Agency at 20 rue de la Chaussee d'Antin, Paris.

4   5

6 MUSICAL FORTUNE TELLER
England, John Dennison 1892 (41x24x27). Have your fortune told and listen to a pleasant tune. This machine is worked by coins - the fairy moves, the owls fly away, the curtain rises and your horoscope appears. It is one of the oldest known coin machines.

7 LE PHENIX (THE PHOENIX)
France, Nau circa 1899 (74x52x29cm). Abel Nau (1858-1936) seems to be the sole French manufacturer of musical slot machines. On this countertop model, which is of excellent quality, it is not the disc that turns but the needle. From all the symbols displayed, only the glass is a winner. The values on the playing cards tell your fortune. This novel presentation could have been inspired by Samuel Nafew's *Improved Horse-Shoe* (1896) or Gustav FW Schultze's *Star* (1896).

Abel Nau knew American manufacturers well, having been the exclusive French importer of the 90's pioneer, The Cowper Machine Company, before becoming a manufacturer himself.

6

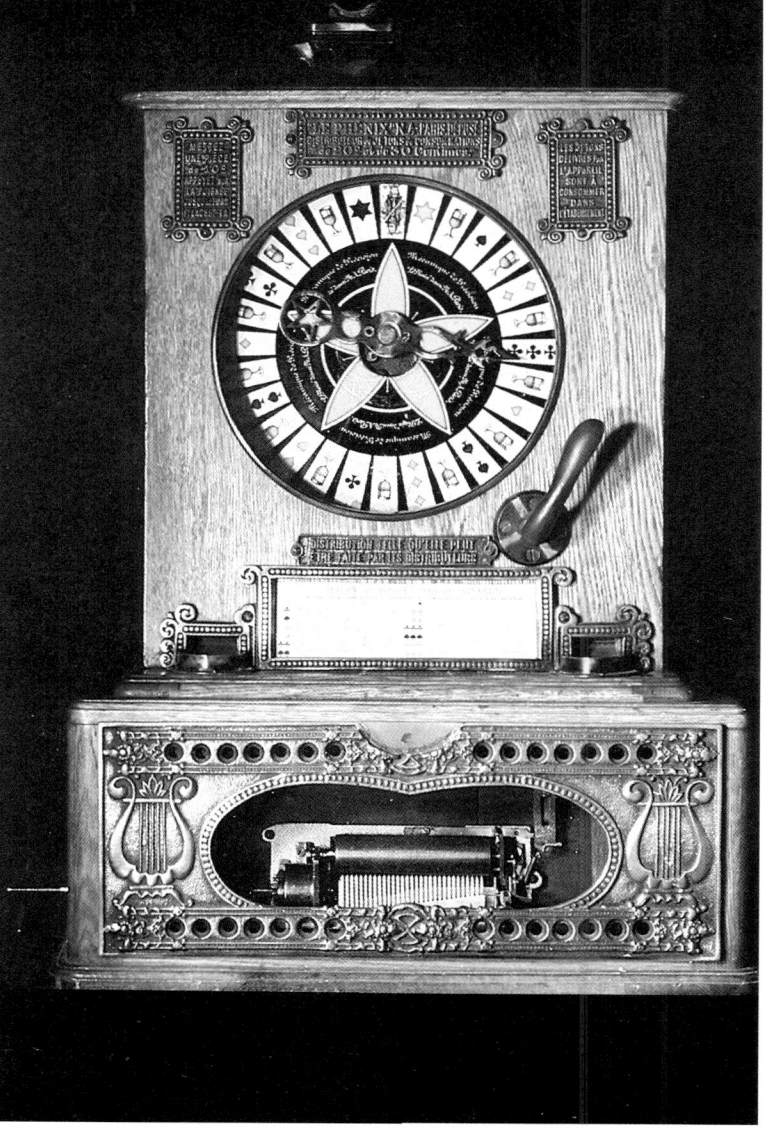
7

Wall Machines

This is a very specific category of slot machines. The game obviously still requires luck but it is no longer the only requirement. The player can use his skill as well to influence the outcome whether for good or bad. These machines are all equipped with an automatic payout system, either coins or tokens, depending upon the legislation in force in the country of use. The common denominator is that they all have one or more balls to be propelled into the winning place. There is a considerable variety of these highly decorative items.

IMPROVED PICKWICK
England, Pessers Moody Wraith and Gurr, 1914 (87x30x18cm) (p 138 fig C). The long, narrow shape makes it look like a vertical mechanical billiard table. The balls are wooden, and the intricate decoration has been most skillfully applied.

ASSORTMENT OF FRENCH WALL MACHINES
1900-1930 (72x46x18cm, on average). Nearly all French manufacturers at the beginning of the automatic era built and sold this type of machine. They are rarely signed so it is difficult to identify the manufacturer from among Angelique, Barlan, Barme, Beraud, Bignell, Braesch, Bussoz, Chapsal, Fritz, Grasset. Lamaziere, Le Dentu, Loubet, Mays, Meyer, Nau, Pasteur, Pierre, Spanagel, etc. This is not really a problem as they are all very decorative, nearly always different and a must for collectors. (p 138 fig A; p 139, figs A,B,C,D & E; p 140, fig C,D and p 148, figs A,E).

JOKER BOUL
France, Courson 1936 (72x46x18cm) (p 140, fig D).

LE BILLARD VERTICAL (VERTICAL BILLIARDS)
Manufacturer unknown, circa 1910 (79x55x20cm)
If you do not lose you can either have another free game, or win, two, three or ten times the sum put in. The ball is wooden. (p 148, fig D).

WIN EASY
England, British Manufacturing Company circa 1930 (43x66x17cm). The ball is about 4cm in diameter. This increase of size over classic machines is debatable as far as aesthetics are concerned, but it was very successful in its appeal to players.

8 LE 12
France, Bussoz, circa 1910 (74x48x19cm). My first machine which I found at the Porte de Clignancourt Flea-market in Paris in 1963. The mechanism is extremely complex: to win you have to get 12 points with 2 balls. This is a very rare machine and there are only 2 known examples. It was a real stroke of luck to be able start off the collection in this way.

9 PIERROT
France, manufacturer unknown, circa 1915 (72x46x18cm). A lovely automatic slot machine. The simplicity of its decoration goes hand in hand with the simplicity of operation. Put in the coin and a ball appears in front of Pierrot's articulated foot. Move the lever and Pierrot kicks the ball. To win the ball has to fall into the centre of the sun. This is the only known example.

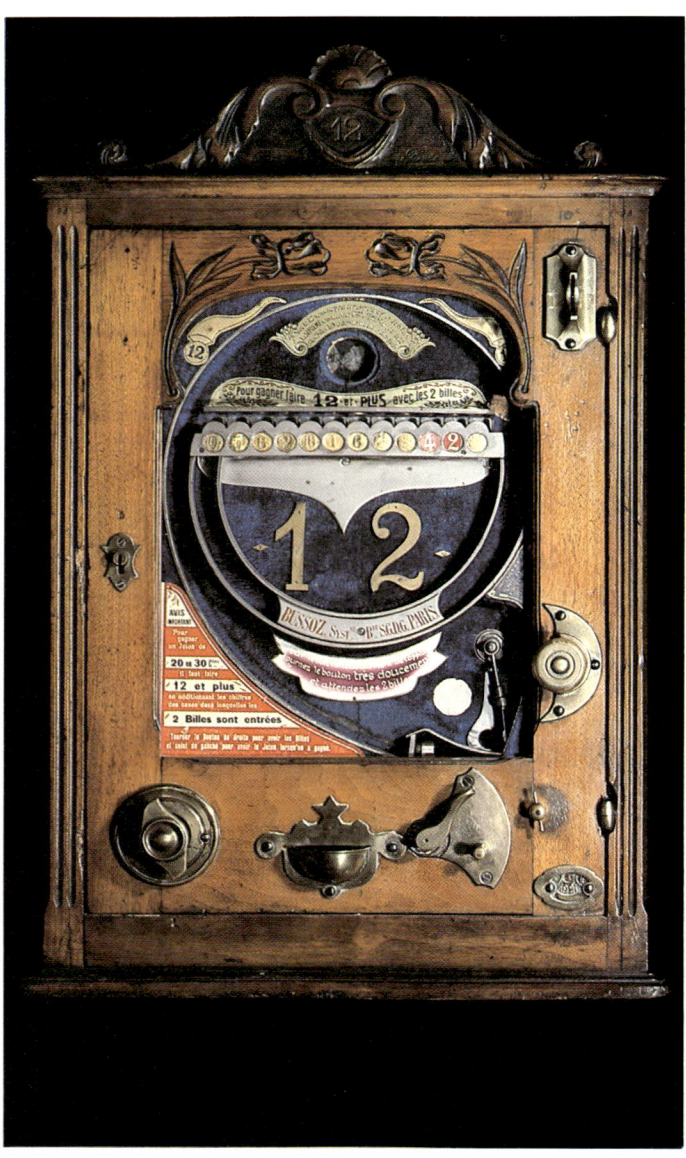

10 LES GUGUSS (THE CLOWNS)
France, Pasteur 1905 (74x51x28cm). This is a real gem. When the coin goes in the slot a ball appears at the Clown's foot. By moving his foot with the lever the player drives the ball into the glass. The next lever controls the arms and the player has to try and throw the ball into the hat. If the ball overshoots the hat, the frog gobbles it up and the game is lost. However if the ball gets into the hat, it rolls along a groove and falls into the pipe which tips under its weight. So the ball returns to the clown's foot and you win a second go and also double the money you put in. The clowns' heads are in coloured cast-iron. This is the only known example.

11 LE COQ PHENIX (THE PHOENIX COCKEREL)
France, Nau 1903 (74x47x18cm) The name Phoenix is found on several quite different machines made by Abel Nau.

11

12 LES FOOTBALLEURS (THE FOOTBALLERS)
Germany, Jentzsch and Meerz circa 1925 (65x48x15cm). An automatic slot machine. Here again it is the player's foot that moves the ball and, to win, the other player has to catch it. The ball is activated by the handle on the left.

13 LE TAXI
France, Beraud circa 1905 (72x47x17cm). A good example of high quality metallic decoration.

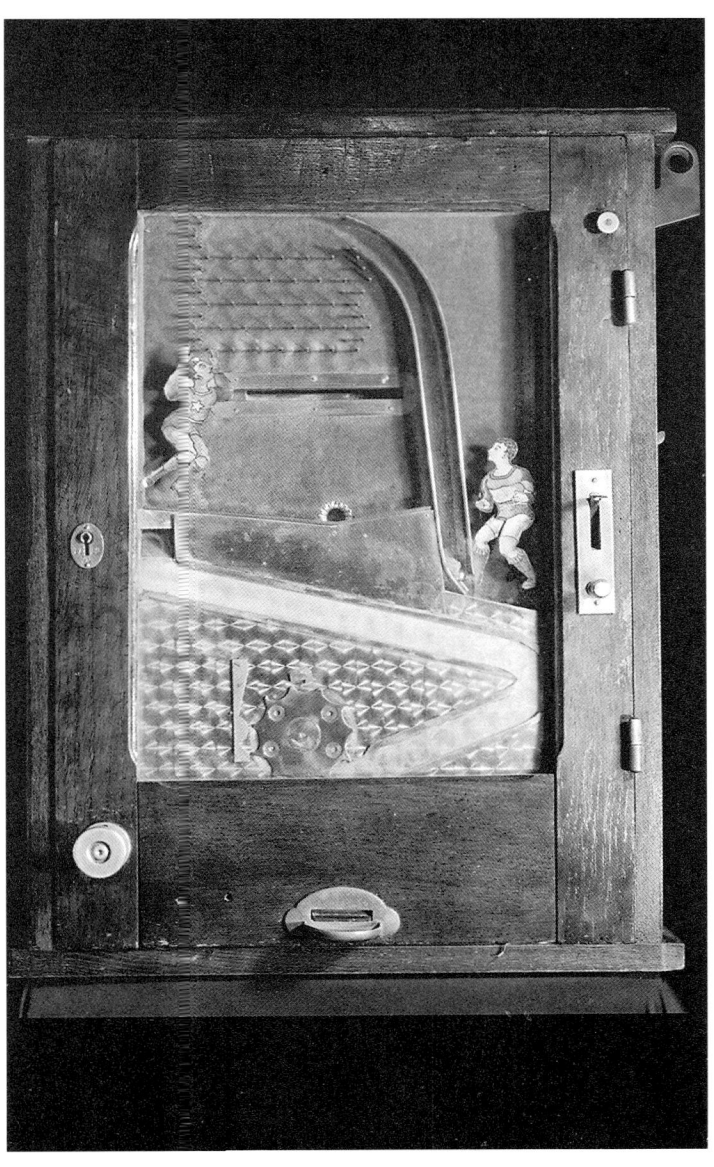

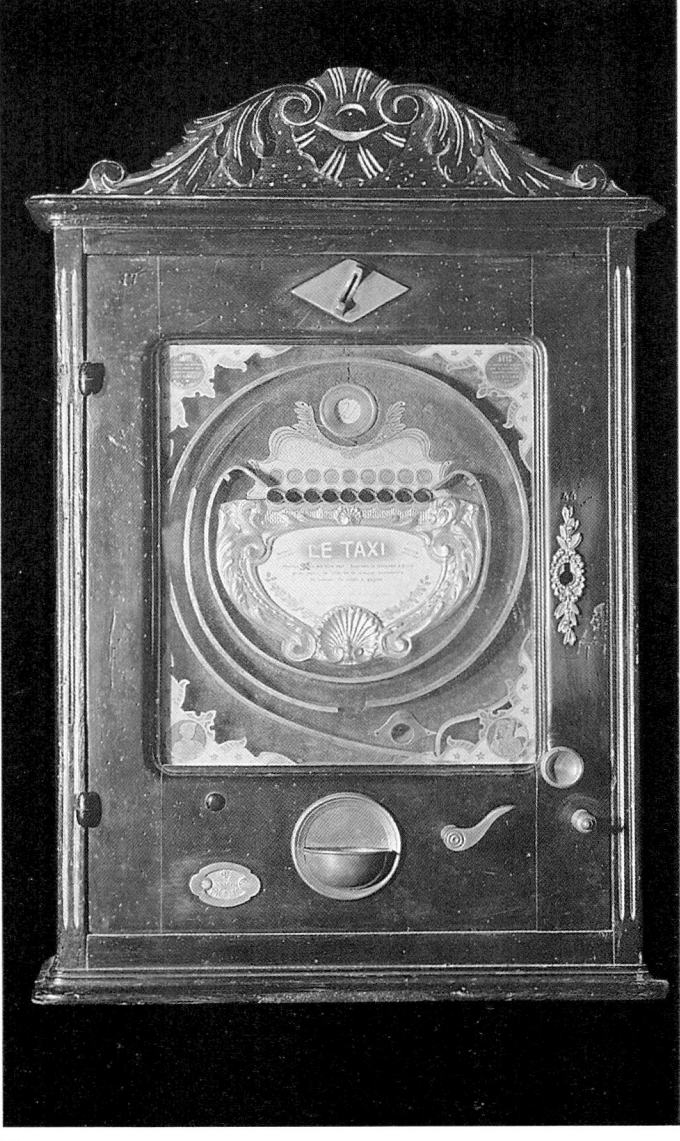

14 LE MILLE (THE BULLSEYE)
France, Bussoz, circa 1910 (74x48x19cm). The extremely complicated mecahnism of the *No 12* made it very expensive and Pierre Bussoz (1872 - 1958) realised that it had to be made more simple. It looks roughly the same, but the wooden case is a little less ornate. You no longer need 12 to win, just to put the ball in the bullseye.

15 BIJOU PICKWICK
Great Britain, Pessers Moody Wraith and Gurr, 1914 (79c47x16cm). A very beautiful, early English wall machine. The balls are made of wood.

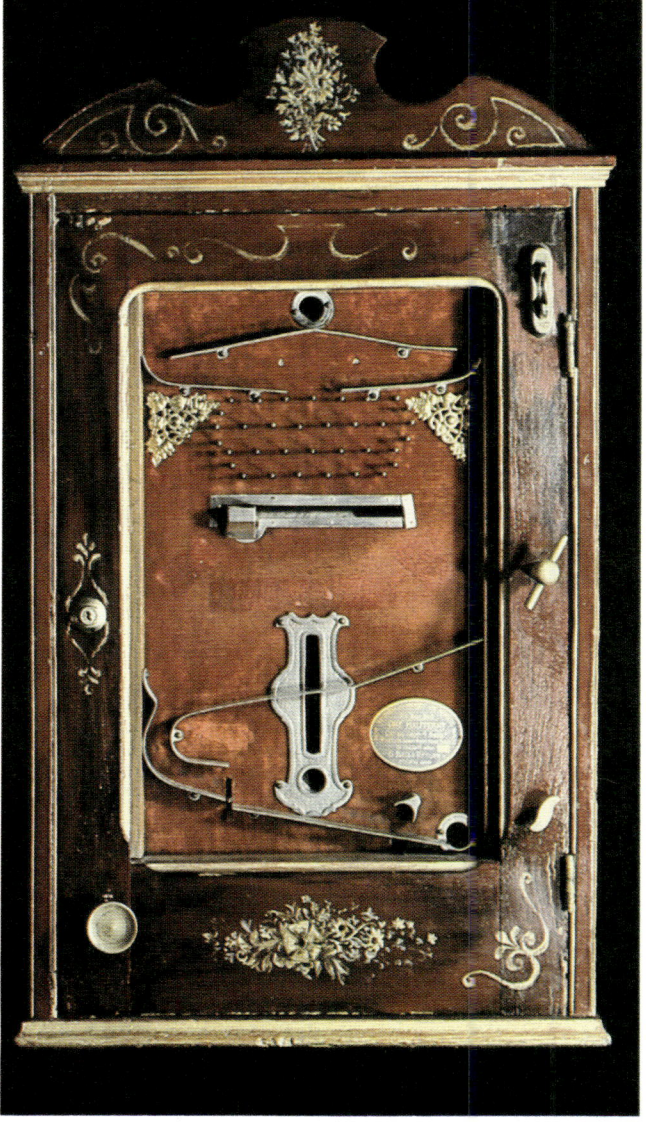

14

15

16 LES TONNEAUX (THE BARRELS)

France, manufacturer unkown circa 1905 (63x48x17cm). Curiously enough, the manufacturer here transformed a machine of skill into a pure game of chance. At the peak of its trajectory the ball goes into a tunnel and then into one of the three barrels. By turning the little button on the right the player is able to put the cup under the barrel of his choice. Then he frees the ball using the lever under the slot. If he has managed to pick the winning barrel, the ball falls into the cup and he wins 3 times his original stake.

17 THE IMPROVED PICKWICK

Great Britain, Handan-Ni, circa 1912 (105x38x19cm). This looks like a mechanical game of billiards but it is played vertically. The aim is to put the ball into the central cup. One of the very few games of skill suited to left handers (the cup can be operated by the left hand).

18 L'ECUREUIL (THE SQUIRREL)

France, manufacturer unknown circa 1903 (60x41x12cm). It is not altogether clear why it is called the Squirrel but no doubt it comes from the action of the ball which, once in play, bounces on the pins. The ribbons which are suspended from the pins seem to be purely decorative.

19 THE CLOWN

Germany, Jentzsch and Meerz, circa 1912 (69x47x16cm). The skill here is to move the clown so that he catches the ball as it drops between the pins. As an added attraction for the players, the manufacturer has incorporated a rotating ball which cleverly gives the impression that the clown himself is moving it.

18

19

20 LE POLO
France, A. Angelique, circa 1903 (70x40x15cm). The balls are wooden. By a stroke of luck the manufacturer can be identified exactly thanks to his publicity material. This very model appeared on an old postcard.

21 BULL DOG
Great Britain, Handan-Ni, circa 1919 (72x52x32cm). The machine is operated by pressing the lever on the left and lifting it to make the ball appear. The handle on the right controls the metal disc. The object of the game is to hold the ball until it falls through the metal pins into the central hole above the bulldog. A fascinating and rare piece.

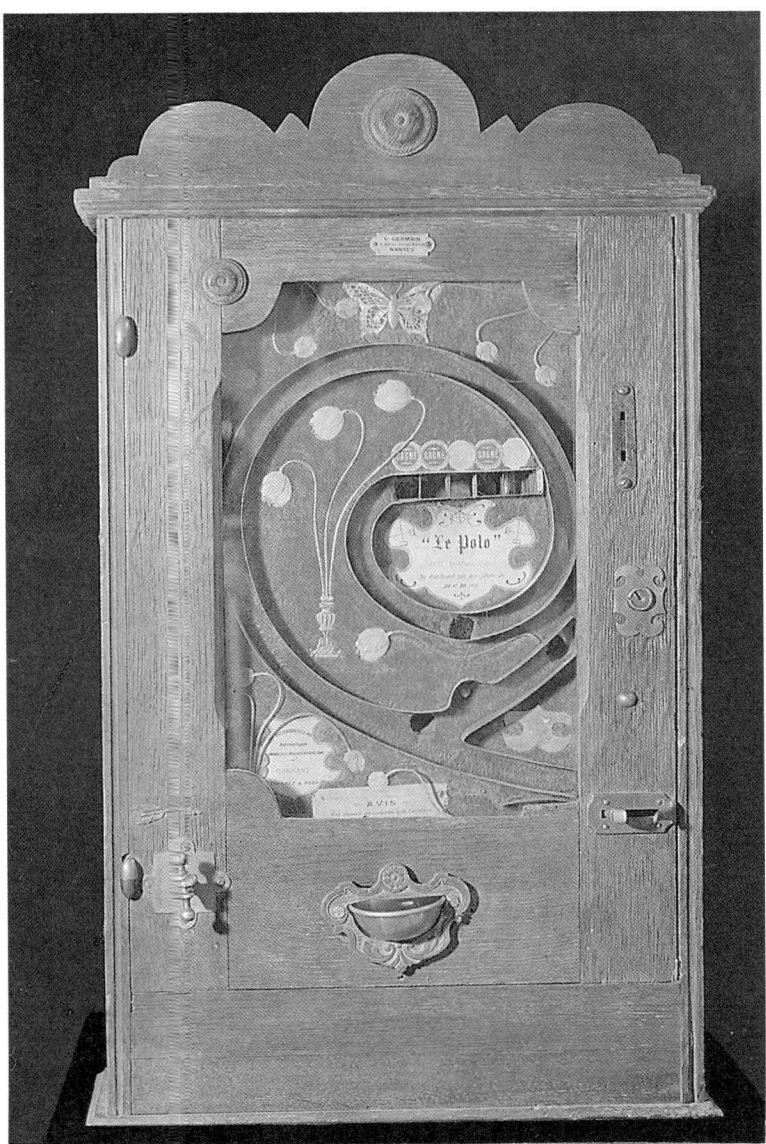

22 LE PORTE-BONHEUR (GOOD LUCK CHARM)

France, manufacturer unkown, circa 1910 (70x42x17cm). This model is very interesting because it has three slots for the coins and every hole is a winner .... providing that the ball goes into the hole chosen by the player before he puts his money in !

23 LE MAGIC

France, Beraud, circa 1910 (54x44x22cm). A beautiful slot machine on two counts - its original design and its ingenious mechanism. The ball has to be shot into one of the winning holes in the row. To prevent the player from winning each and every time, the winning hole, indicated by a black disc, changes position.

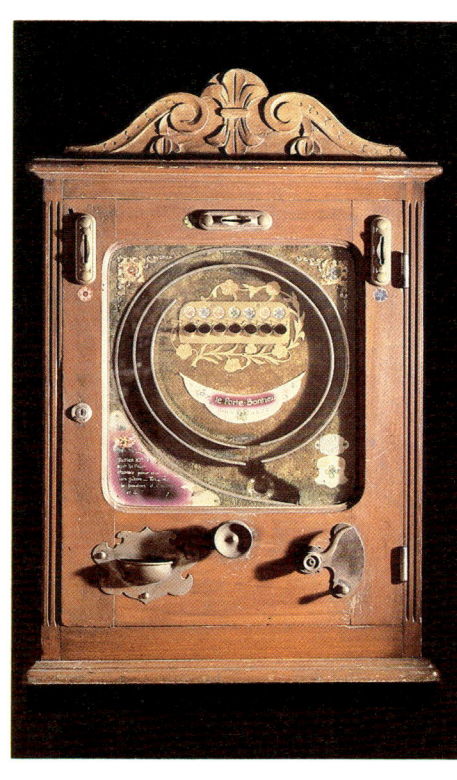

22

23

Special Slot Machines

This nomenclature is applied to all machines operated by the introduction of a coin and which have a more or less automatic pay-out. This might be either coins or tokens depending on the current legislation. Classifying by type is difficult and anyway fairly artificial. In the book we have used seven categories: musical machines, ball machines (which as a general rule are made of cast iron or brass plated with nickel or chrome), jack-pots, roulettes, targets, triple reels and specials. This last group encompasses all those slot machines which do not fit neatly into any of the other six groups. Their external appearance may be very varied but the majority of them have the same reel or disc mechanics - even if the reel is often just a horizontal or vertical plate. In the following selection of special machines there are some very fine examples of the craft.

LA COMETE
USA, Mills, 1906 (32x34x27cm). Halley's comet no longer being such a novelty, this designer tried to improve the situation by replacing the star symbols with the head of a beautiful girl and a very French cockerel. Love, that inexhaustable and irresistible theme, easily attracts players - and makes more money for the owner (p 153, fig C).

SWEEPSTAKES
USA, Rock-Ola, 1935. This is a horse race game with eight runners paying out chewing gum (p 148 fig B)

24 LE SOURIRE (THE SMILE)

France, manufacturer unknown, circa 1910 (64x57x24cm). Both Galle and Mucha would have applauded this Art Nouveau decor in the pure style of the Nancy School. On the other hand, the disc illustrated with early designs of aeroplane is hardly a success, despite dating from the same period.

25 THE TIGER

USA, Caille, 1905 (47x37x31cm). In 1905 suddenly everyone seemed to be copying everyone else's designs. This variant of The Tiger was manufactured by Caille specifically for the French market.

24

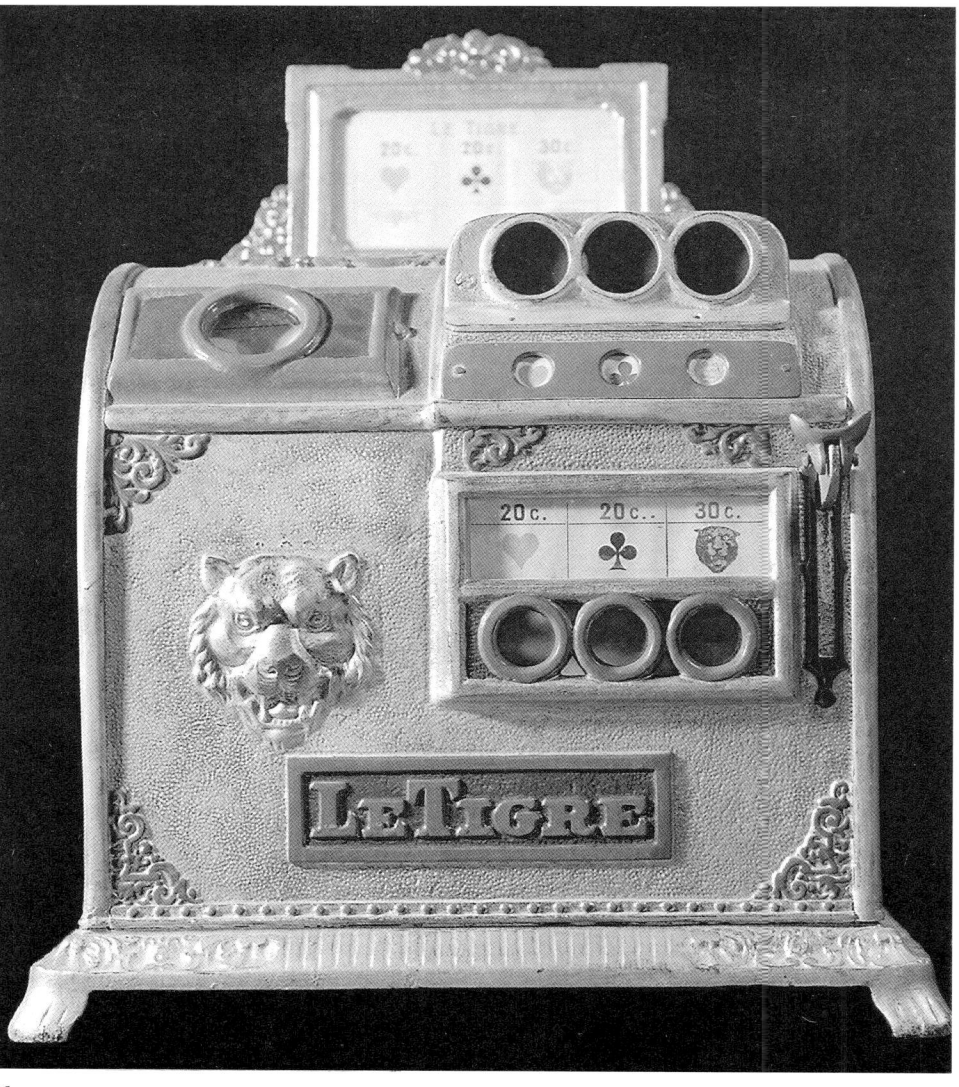

25

26 THE COMET
   USA, Mills, 1906 (32x34x27cm). Many astronomers at the beginning of the century were predicting the end of the world for May 19th 1910, the estimated date for Halley's Comet to collide with Earth. Luckily they miscalculated and the comet just came close to earth - however Mills made a fortune with this aptly named machine.

27 LES PETITS CHEVAUX (LITTLE HORSES)
   France, Nau, 1905 (42x44x28cm). A French version of Mills' *Elk*, the main difference being the pay-out part which is not unlike the big music machines in appearance.

26

27

28 LA GRENOUILLERE (FROG'S POND)
 France, manufacturer unknown, circa 1910 (44x37x25cm). The graceful curves of this machine clearly show the influence of Art Nouveau. The mechanism is identical with *Monte-Carlo* and *Old Man Bidard* apart from one simple difference: it's no longer a ball which indicates the winning colour on the front mounted disc, but a business-like opening in the back of the machine. The disc or flange has simply been repositioned and enlarged.

29 LE PERE BIDARD (OLD MAN BIDARD)
 France, manufacturer unknown, circa 1918 (43x37x27cm). This gem of primitive art deserves the closest attention. The coin is put down one of the chimneys and the winning tokens come out through the sleeping dog's kennel. Above this, on the right, two doves bill and coo. At one side a heart has been cut into the lavatory door with somebody sweeping inside. On the facade is old man Bidard himself, true forerunner of the comic-strip character, announcing the merits of the machine.

28

29

44

30 LIBERTY COMMERCIAL
   France ?, manufacturer unknown circa 1930 (56x35x33cm). There are only two known examples of this machine. The exceptionally fine Art Deco design is moulded in iron.

31 THE FILM STARS
   Great Britain, Tom Boland revamp based on the Mills mechanism, 1948 (64x45x37cm). A cleverly presented single reel machine in the characteristic style of three-reel machines. The usual fruits are replaced by world-famous film stars. Just change the pictures to update the image - Rita Hayworth and John Wayne conjure up the 1950's.

32 LE HARAS (THE STUD FARM)
   France, New Polyphon Supply Company, circa 1905 (47x33x29cm). According to Abel Nau's son, this would appear to be a copy of his father's *Little Horses*, a copy built in Germany for export to France.

31

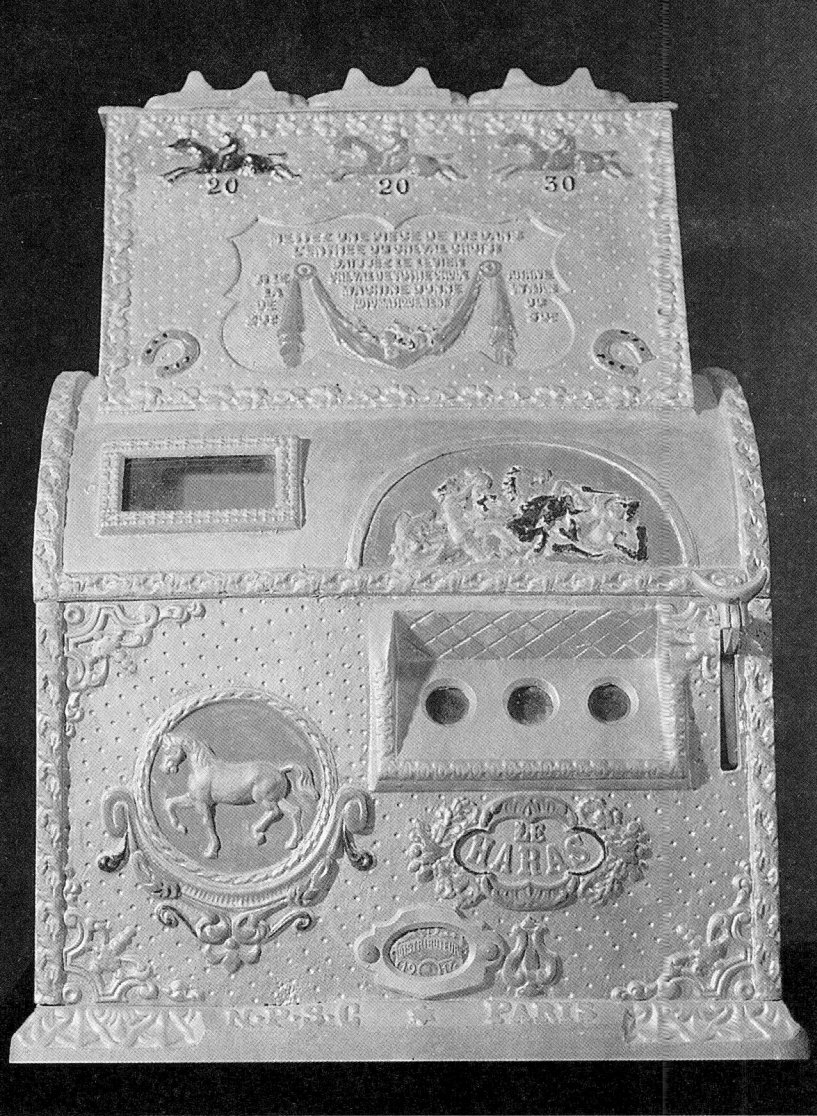

32

33 BOXOMAT

Germany, Boxomat, circa 1930 (153x74x56cm). This is an exceptional example of the purest Art Deco style with a clear cubist influence and is the only known example.

34 LES AVIONS (AEROPLANES)

France, manufacturer unknown, 1935 (51x42x42cm). When you put your money in, the planes turn. Then you must manipulate the throttle so that the coin falls precisely into the grooved piece supporting the planes. If you manage it, your coin is returned together with a drinks token. Difficult but good fun.

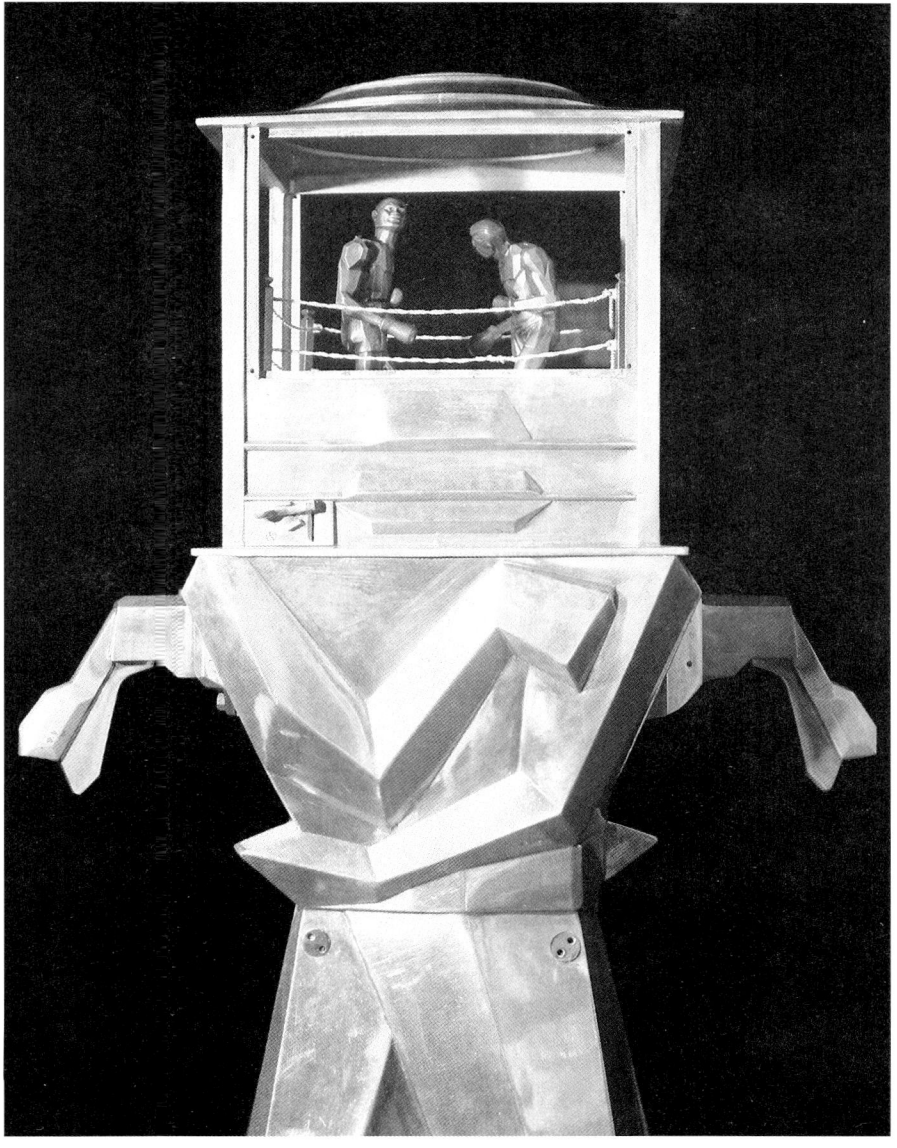

33

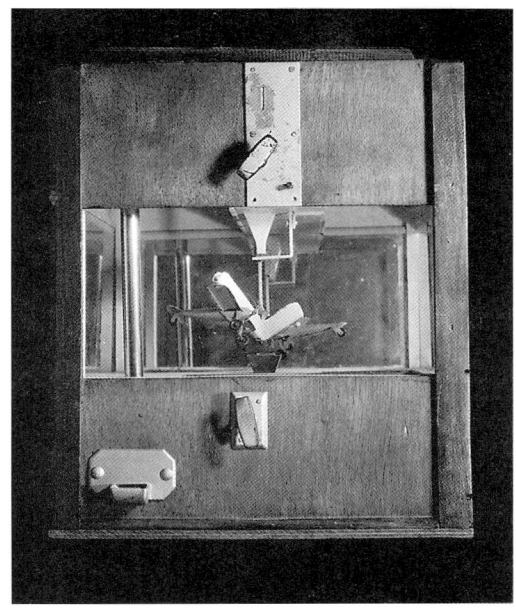

34

35 MONTE CARLO

France, manufacturer unknown, circa 1905 (44x31x23cm). This is an exact scale replica of the facade of the Monte Carlo casino. This machine has the same mechanism as *Frog's Pool* and *Old Man Bidard* and the design of all three is possibly by the same artist. These superb models are not mentioned in any catalogue, text or archive, their origin remains a complete mystery.

36 THE COMMERCIAL

USA, Caille, 1905 (63x40x24cm). The mechanism here is as complex as in the big music machines, but the manufacturer has tried to reduce the size so that it can be used on bar tops. The printed disc on the front could be changed so that customers would think that the machine had been replaced by a new model.

37 LE PASSE-PARTOUT (YOUR FORTUNE)

France, manufacturer unknown, circa 1920 (31x26x18cm). Each winter showmen repainted all their machines. The more talented ones gave us this style of primitive art, known nowadays as fairground art.

35

36

37

38 HORSE RACE
USA, Foresty, 1933 (47x41x38cm). Here you choose your horse and place your bet on the selected number. The horses go round and round and when they stop you hope it will be on your winning number. It is a wooden machine with a metal turntable.

39 PACE'S RACES
USA, Pace, 1934 (93x111x50cm). The biggest and most complex slot machine of the period. An electric motor operates 27 bellows to form a vacuum in 100 metres of fusing which then sucks the horses towards the finishing line. The possible pay out on each horse changes during the race thanks to a perforated paper roll - what an achievement for the 1930's - allowing you to win two to twenty times your original bet. The machine is not that rare but it is difficult to restore, and there are only two working examples to be found in France.

38

39

40 LE GLOBE
France, Ma cuit, 1934 (103x52x42cm).

41 LE JOCKEY
France, Miguel, 1934 (165x50x34cm). This superb machine, 1.80m high, was invented and patented by Louis Miguel. It is the Derby, with betting on one of three colours. The horses start to turn as soon as the handle is operated. There is an automatic payment of winnings.

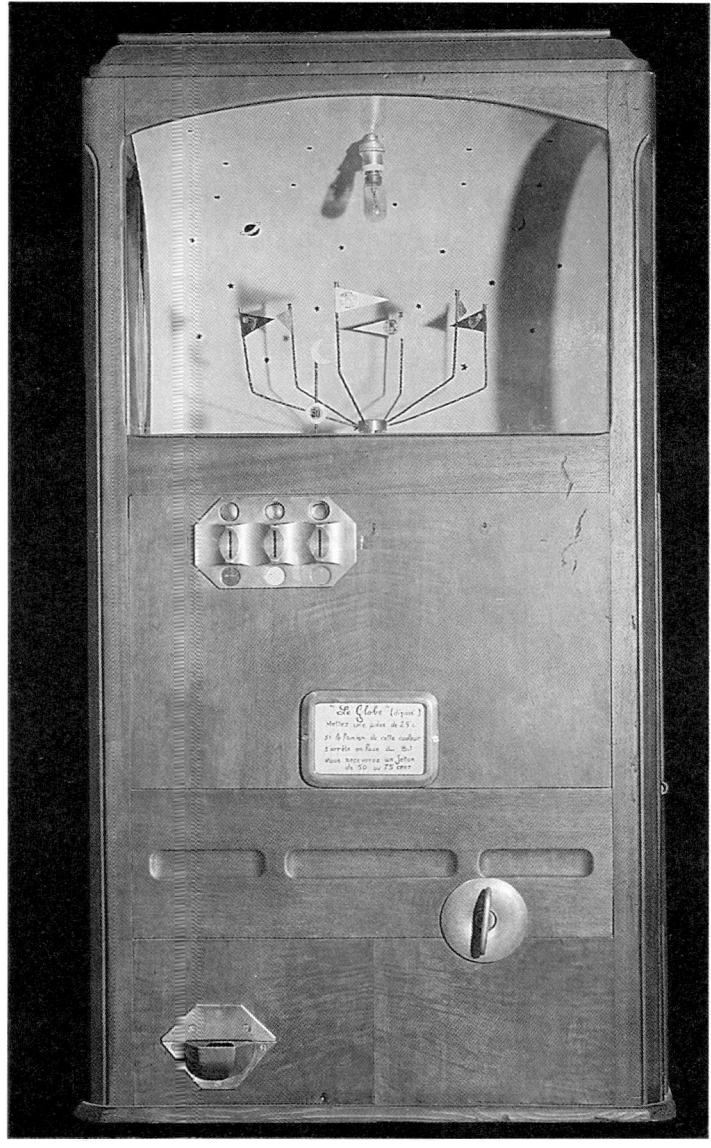

40

41

42 MATADOR

France, Caille, circa 1905 (42x36x32cm). This polychromed iron machine is decorated with a vivid scene from the bull ring, which was the latest vogue in the early part of the century. However the game has no connection with bull-fighting at all. Matador was a variation of dominoes in which a player had to always score seven points to start, and to win. This is the only known example.

43 THE ELK

USA, Mills, 1905 (48x32x27cm). Elk hunting was very fashionable at this time. Note the wealth of detail on this cast iron machine, copied by Mills from the previous year's model made by Paupa and Hochreim.

42

44 LE MILLE (BULLSEYE)
France, manufacturer unknown, 1935 (70x35x20cm). A fascinating game of skill in which you have to lift the ball right up, balancing it on two teeth controlled by two handles. But these handles are tricky to operate because they turn in opposite directions simultaneously. To make matters worse, electric shocks were sent out at the same time. Only two known examples.

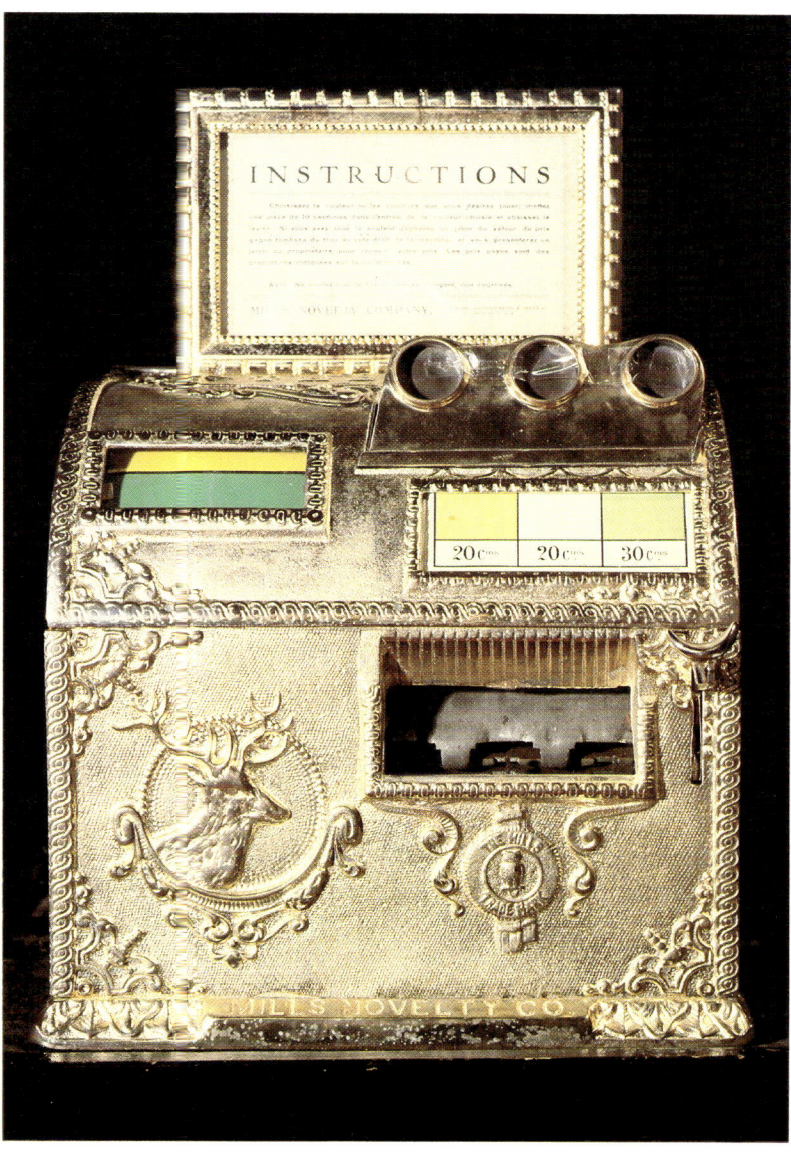

43

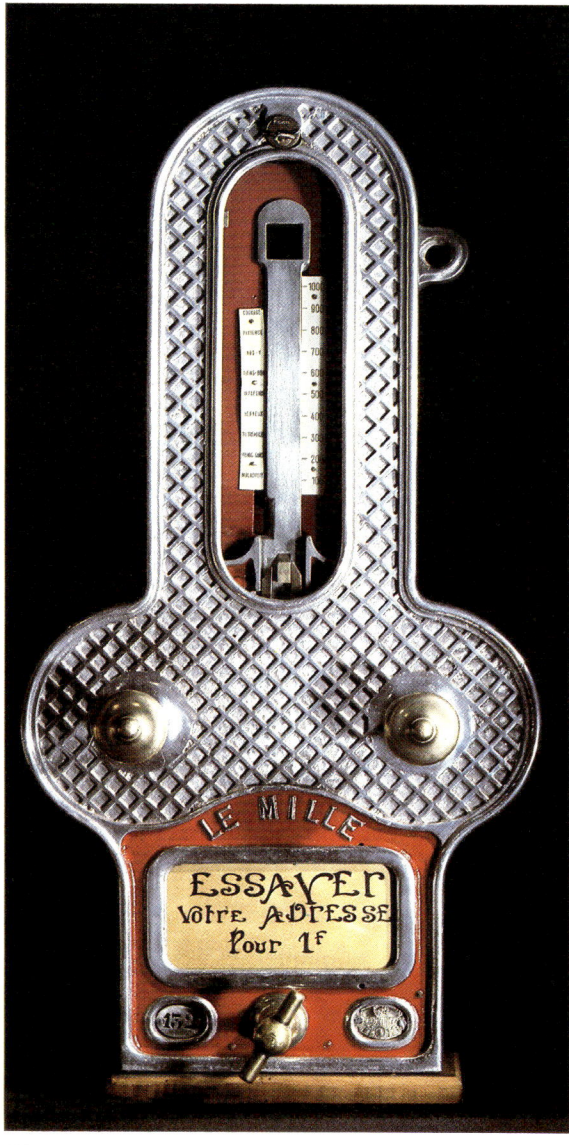

44

45 BONES
USA, Buckley, 1936 (31x42x29cm). Here the mechanism, which is as tricky as it is sophisticated, imitates the real game of craps. Note the way the word BONES appears to be made of bones.

46 ROLLING POKER
USA, Blanchard, 1935. (55x44cm). The glass front shows the complex mechanism. If the three balls fall onto the same colour, the winner takes all. Each lever at the side selects one colour. This is the only known example.

45

46

Drop Case Machines

What could be more fascinating for the player than to watch the his coin falling and bouncing on the pins before coming to rest in the win or lose slot? As he follows its progress he is convinced it is his skill influencing the outcome and nothing to do with the way the machine has been fixed. There are not very many models of this type with a visible chute where we can actually watch the coins cascading down.

CAGNOTTE (JACKPOT)
France, manufacturer unkown, circa 1930 (20x47x29cm) (p 140, fig A).

LA CASCADE (WATERFALL)
Germany, possibly Jentzsch and Meerz, circa 1930 (70x47x16cm) (p 140, fig B).

47 CARLO
USA, Clawson Machine Co, 1894 (60x38x27cm). This represents a very important stage in the history of slot machines. The game is based upon an accumulation of coins which are automatically released - the fore-runner of the jack-pot. It was not for another 30 years that this mechanism was adopted for the triple-drum fruit machine inappropriately called jack-pots in France.

48 CRICKET
USA, Mills, 1904 (173x60x33cm). The most beautiful of the jackpot machines. Once the coin is inserted, the handle at the side of the game throws it tumbling across onto the pins. With plenty of luck it might come to rest above a slot full of other people's money. Turning the little wheel on the right releases this jackpot.

49 UNIC
France, manufacturer unknown, 1895 (75x43x10cm). A surprisingly flat machine in Henry II style, which could win you double or triple the amount put in. This is the only known example.

47

48

49

50 LA PUCE (THE FLEA)
   Germany, Jentzsch and Meerz 1928 (76x46x16cm).

51 LE SPHINX
   France, Automatique DL circa 1930 (68x39x15cm). Once the coin was inserted, you turned the button at the top of the machine which shook the plate up and down.

52 SOLEIL (THE SUN)
   France, manufacturer unknown, circa 1910 (65x49x14cm). Here for once with the central V shaped wedges, this unidentified manufacturer has tried to give the player a helping hand.

53 L'ELITE
   Germany, Jentzsch and Meerz circa 1930 (77x47x16cm).

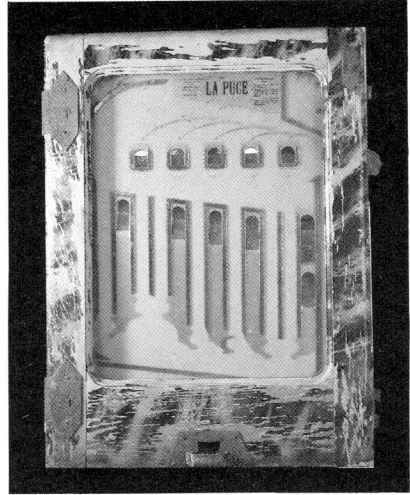
50

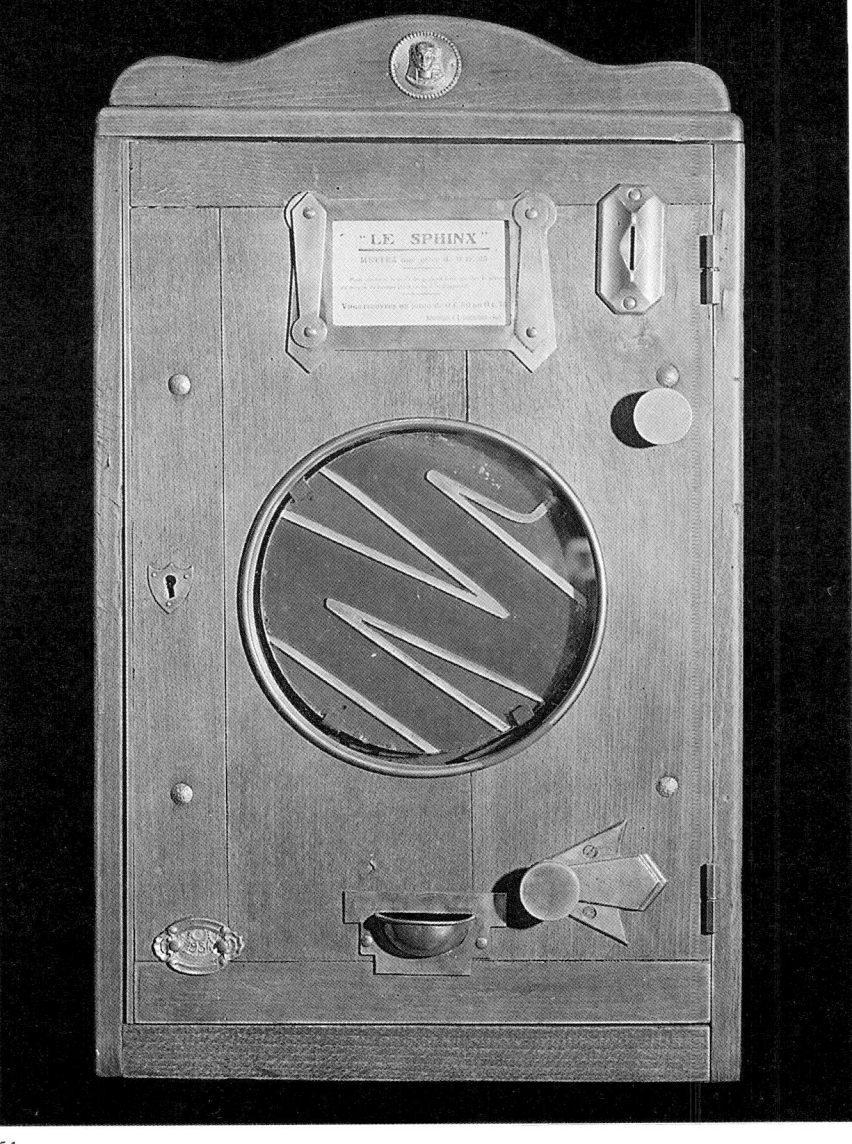
51

52

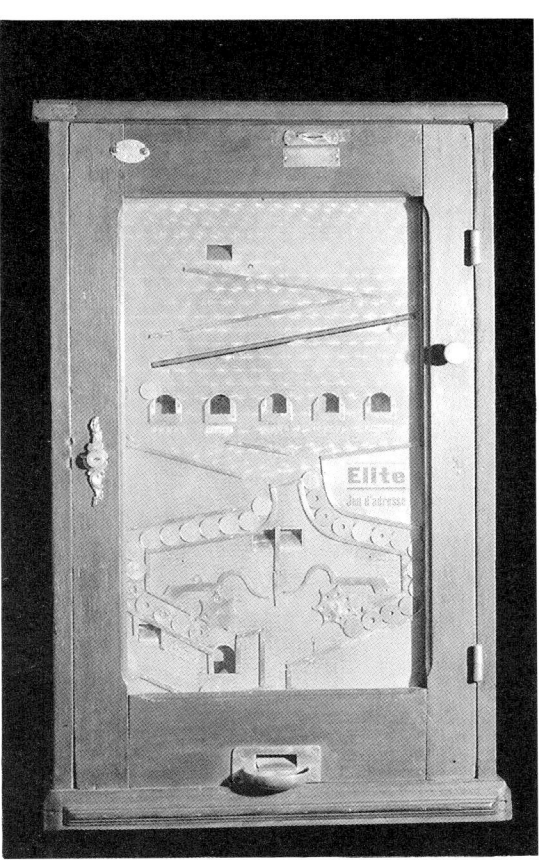

53

59

54 LITTLE DREAM

USA, Caille, 1901 (54x35x24cm). Mills and Caille made such similar machines that their models could only be told apart by the name on the lever or the key-plate. This machine is another milestone in the mechanical development of the slot machine, introducing tilt. If the player tries to shake the machine to guide the falling coin, a counterweight releases a toothed rod which stops the coin from finding a winning hole. However most machines were not so equipped, and this variant is uncommon.

55 LE PHENIX

France, Pierre Nau, circa 1905 (66x43x15cm). It is the coin itself that falls and bounces off the pins, watched by the anxious player who prays that his money will disappear into the winning hole.

54

55

56 JACKPOT
Great Britain possibly Chubbs Automatics, 1930 (83x51x19cm). The name Jackpot is interesting. It literally means Jack's store, but at first the manufacturers only used the word jacks, not jackpot. This term came to be applied generally to any kind of three reel fruit machine.

57 LE CHIEN SAVANT (CLEVER DOG)
France or Germany, circa 1925 (72x47x20cm). The handle at bottom left moves the dog which has a top-hat in its mouth. You have to catch the coin in the hat and then guide it to the right into the winning hole.

56

57

Roulettes

The distinctive feature of this family of machines is its one wheel that is a disc or a plate which turns in lottery style or, more precisely, like a roulette wheel. This wheel is divided into numbered segments each with a diferent symbol such as plants, glasses or bottles. The winning segment is indicated by a marker, often an arrow, ball or person, when the wheel stops turning. These spinning dial games were amongst the earliest categories of coin freed gambling games. They were to be superceded in popularity by the advent of the 3 reeler.

LES 3 TETES (THREE HEADS)
France, manufacturer unknown, circa 1910 (70x46x20cm). Classic roulette with very special metal body decorated by three heads in relief. Origin unknown. A rather splendid devil pops up to stop the wheel. (p 147, fig C)

SELECT ROULETTE
France, Bussoz, circa 1925 (72x46x20cm). Its owner, doubtless a real admirer of classic roulette, replaced the two original pointers with two discs. As a result there were many less wins than with ordinary roulette. The mechanics are quite complex. (p 143, fig F)

LA BOULE D'OR (GOLDEN BALL)
France, Bussoz, 1923 (74x46x20cm), The numbers 666 or 999 are the winning combinations. (p 143, fig D)

58 LA ROULETTE
France, Bussoz, 1910 (75x51x18cm). Pierre Bussoz (1872 - 1958) built his first roulette in 1910. Twenty years later with 4,800 machines in use and with more than 80 employees, he became the top man of French automatics. A choice of three colours - blue, yellow or red - allowed a win of two or three times the outlay. The player puts the coin into the slot corresponding to the colour chosen and turns the knob below on the right. Straight away an indicator shows the colour chosen to avoid any argument later. At the same time the wheel spins rapidly on its axis whilst the little man slowly climbs until he stops the disc in the desired spot. Winnings are paid automatically through the little cup below.

59 LA ROULETTE MAYS
France, Mays, circa 1900 (75x50x22cm). Adrien Mays (1857 - 1923) engineer, invented prodigiously during the last quarter of the 19th Century, going by all the medals he was awarded. The most curious patent was for a safety-pin making machine. In 1885 he turned his interest to slot machines. This machine is his third prototype, the side lever being replaced by a handle in the front.

58

59

60 LA MERVEILLEUSE

France, Bussoz, circa 1905 (66x38x14cm). Certain models more or less the same as this are signed Beraud. It seems mysterious but anyway this machine has an ingenious and superbly precise mechanism.

61 LE NOTRE (OURS)

USA, Caille circa 1905 (70x47x19cm). The Caille Brothers Company managed to come up with an interesting variation - they placed the disc at the back so that all the moving parts were easily visible behind the glass door. No doubt they hoped that the French name would make it attractive in the French market. Unfortunately, this name was grammatically incorrect and meant nothing to the French which probably accounts for there being only two known examples today!

60

61 (détail)

61

62 IRIS
Germany, Jentzsch and Meerz, circa 1925 (80x63x21cm). It is well known that the Germans copied Bussoz, but they cleverly called it Iris, a name recognised internationally, unlike the Caille Brothers and Le Notre.

63 LA ROULETTE NOUVELLE (THE NEW ROULETTE)
France, Nau, 1901 (58x45x26cm). Pierre-Abel Nau (1858 - 1936) began by selling American Cowper Machine Company slot-machines in the 1890's. Following their success, he branched out into manufacturing and produced the Phoenix roulette with a side-lever, which he soon replaced by a handle in the front. The New Roulette was his last machine based on this principle.

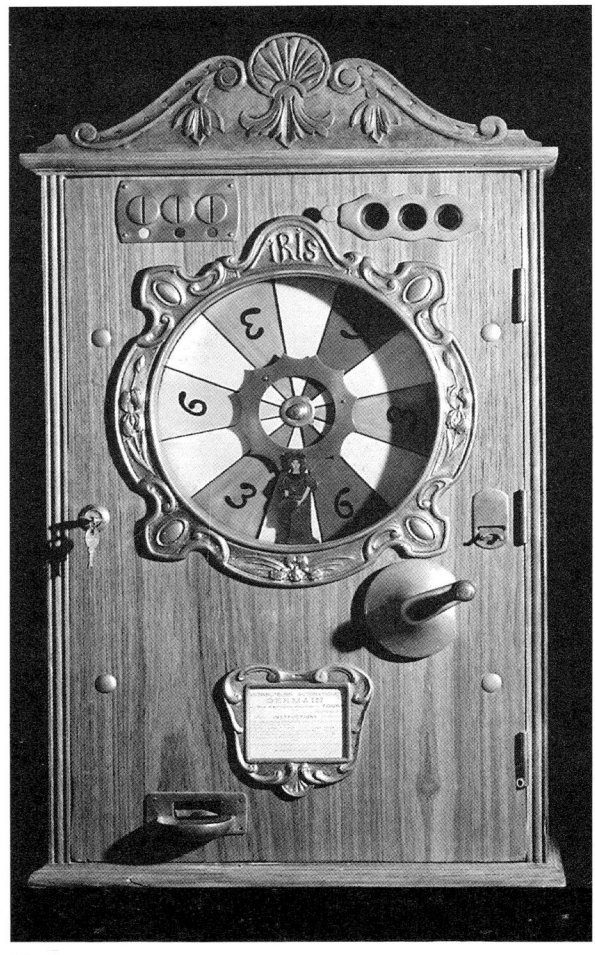

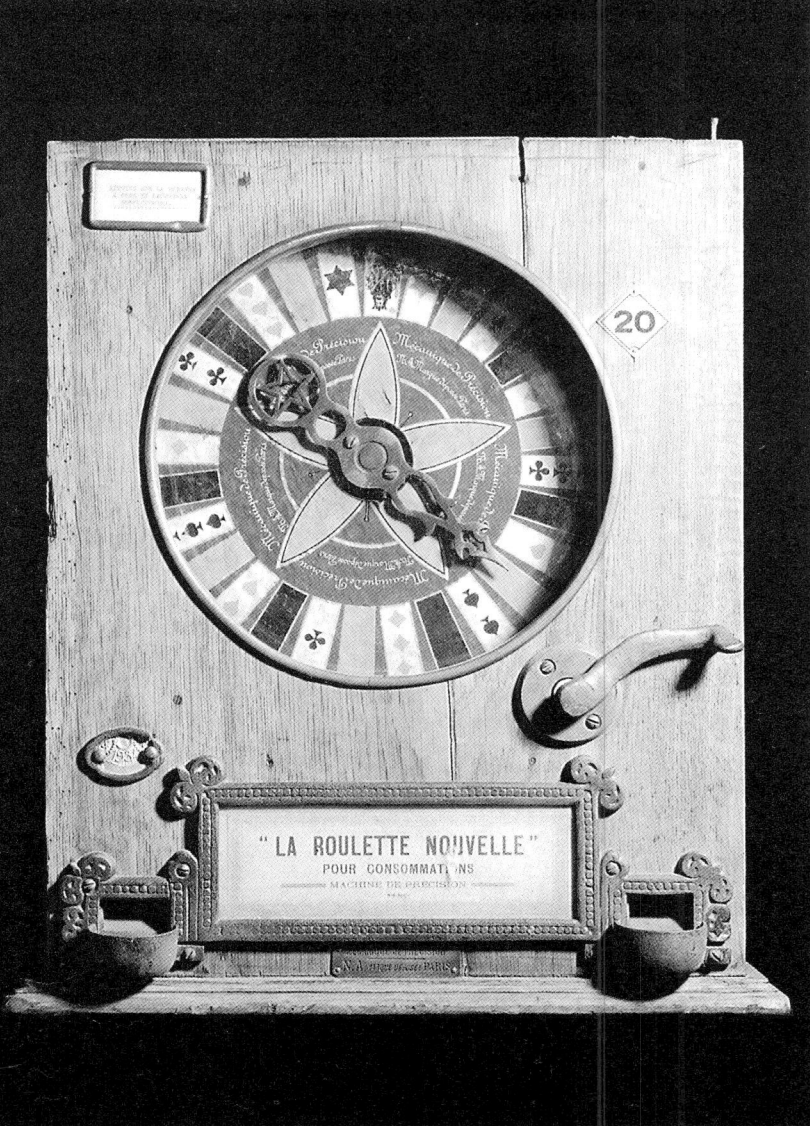

64 LA TRIPLETTE

France, manufacturer unknown, circa 1905 (70x48x19cm). 3 roulettes in one - who could ask for more? This is the only known example and its mechanism is incomplete.

65 ROUGE ET NOIRE (SCARLET AND BLACK)

France, Pierre Nau, circa 1905 (66x44x20cm). When the money is put in, the winning colour is displayed in the window on the right, and a turn of the handle spins the marker.

66 LA GAULOISE
France, Braesch, 1905 (74x60x20cm). No holds were barred in France where they copied each other all the time.

67 LA MUSICIENNE (2nd version)
France, Mays, circa 1895 (65x42x21cm).

68 LA BELOTE MONACO
France, Bussoz, 1922 (73x46x21cm). Bussoz' Belote machine modified by another operator.

69 SELECT ROULETTE

France, Bussoz, circa 1920 (72x46x20cm). Here Bussoz' inspiration seems to be American in origin. The Anthony Co built a machine on the same principle called *The Eclipse* in 1893! The player chose one of two colours and the two hands contra-rotated. To win they both had to stop on the same colour, but fortunately not necessarily in the same position.

70 ROULETTES BUSSOZ

France, 1901-1937 (average 72x46x20cm). Like any serious manufacturer Bussoz kept up with styles and art, keeping his roulettes up to date. He also had a variety of well-known characters to stop the disc: Fernandel, Dranhem, Josephine Baker, Gendarmes, Russian Guards, Judges and Boxers were shown in many positions - from the front, in profile, with arms crossed, fists raised and so on.

There are models in the style of the Belle Epoque, some from the 1920s, others from the 1930s, Bussoz really was the man of 10,000 roulettes. More of these can be seen on page 143 figs A & B. Also page 147 figs A, B, D & E.

69

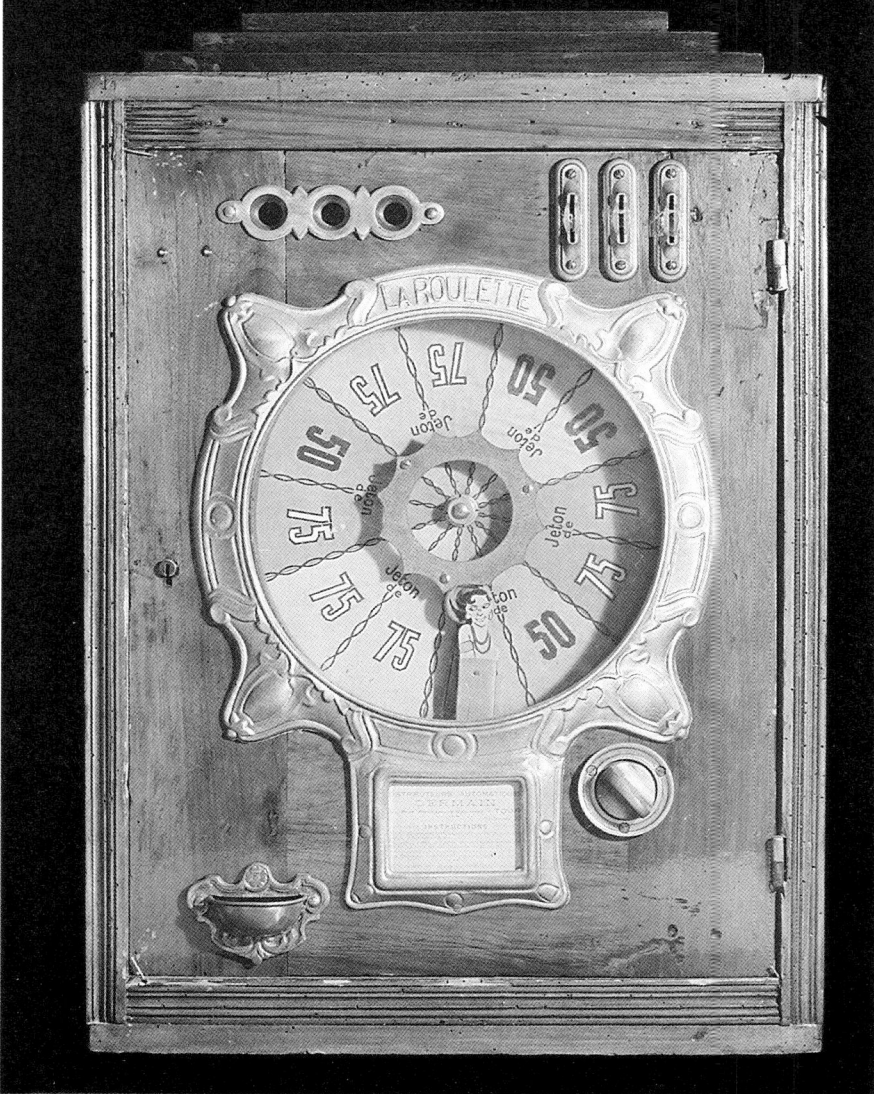

70

71 LE DERBY
France, Holding Automatic, 1928 (65x50x23cm). Horse racing was in fashion; the society ladies of the day went to the weigh-in so a manufacturer produced a personalised roulette with horses shown in raised relief. Money was put on a certain colour as usual.

72 LA MUSICIENNNE
France, Mays, circa 1895 (64x41x18cm). One of the oldest known French slot-machine. Put in a coin and depress the lever on the side. The hand rotates quickly suddenly stopping on the winning or losing symbol.

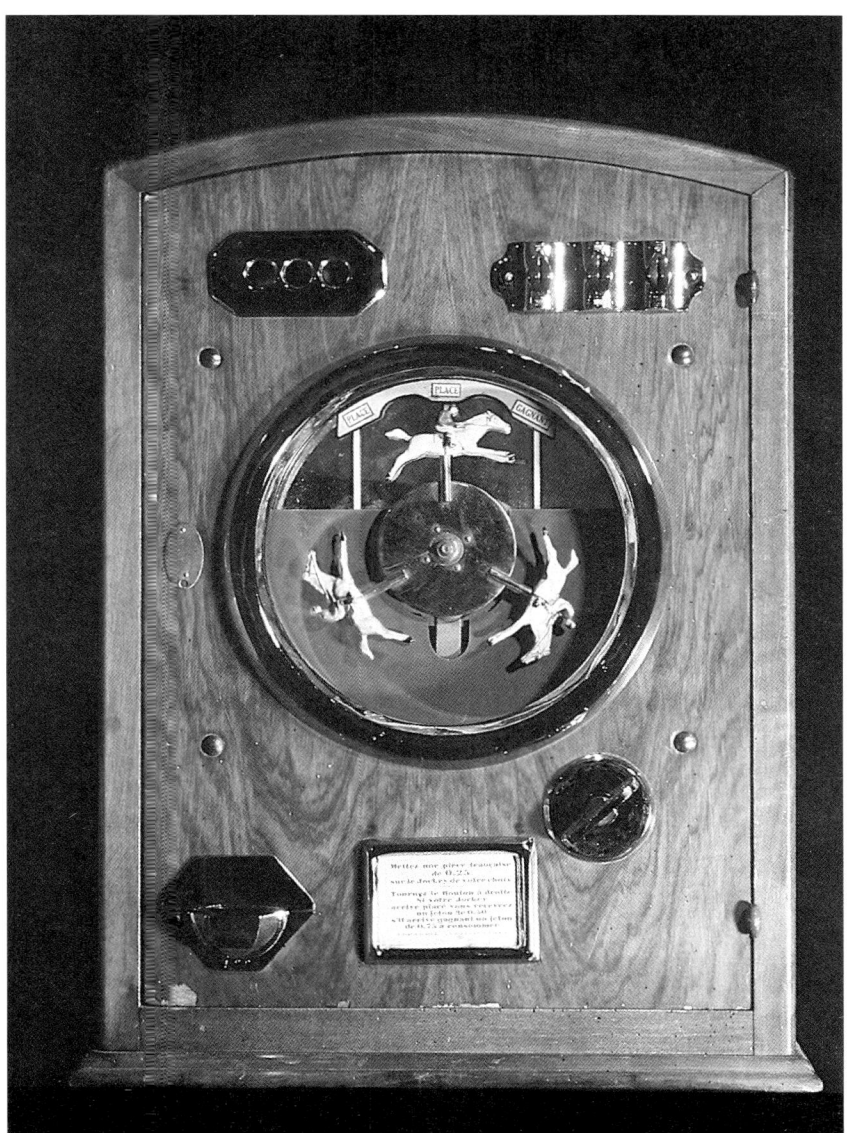

71

72

73 LA ROULETTE DE LA BROCANTEUSE D'AMOUR (THE LOVE DEALER'S ROULETTE)

France, Braesch 1899 (68x49x21cm). An apocryphal story has it that in Paris at the beginning of the century Victorine Tillard ran a brothel-bar at 4 Place Pereire called the Love Dealer. A somewhat indiscreet insight into her life and the passionate esteem in which she was held, is shown by the 800 postcards addressed to her between 1901 and 1904. Not that discretion was one of her virtues! She adapted a roulette machine to fit in with the ambience of her *house* simply replacing the numbers by photos of her girls. What is more, when a customer left one of the girls, if he played the roulette and the hand pointed to the photo of that same girl, he had champagne on the house. For those uncertain which girl to choose, the hand of fate could make the decision for them.

74 MEPHISTO

France, Bussoz, circa 1920 (75x62x20cm). A beautifully painted, showground style Bussoz roulette. Maybe an invitation for Mephistopheles to join in the reckless gambling.

73

74

75 ROULETTE SERPENT

France, possibly Bussoz, circa 1905 (86x58x20cm). The door is cast iron and brass, not wood. This is the original front despite the fact that it was found by pure chance some 800km from the rest of the machine.

76 LA BOUTEILLE

France, manufacturer unknown, circa 1895 (61x43x15cm). This is the only known example and the maker cannot be identified. The wheel turns and if the longest hand stops on a glass, you win double your money. On a bottle, you get a triple win, but between the two, nothing at all. Note the quality of etching on the mirror below and the integral carving of three women on the decorated bronze handle.

75

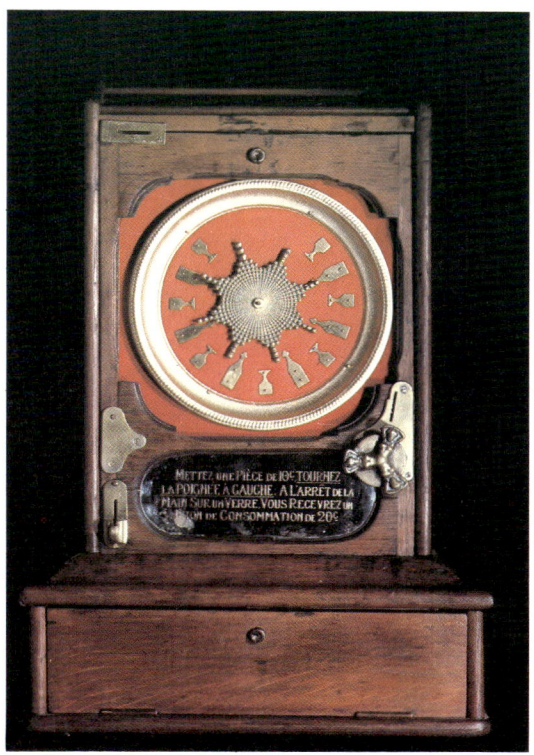

76

Shooting Machines

At the beginning of the century most players were men. Some manufacturers went beyond the hunting theme and brought out slot machines based on shooting galleries and used a pistol as an integral part of the machine.

TIR FRITZ
France, manufacturer unknown, circa 1910 (145x27x112cm). This machine is not coin-operated, but was commonly found at the beginning of the century at village fairs and amusement arcades. The rifle fired real 5.5mm bullets. This machine, including the stand and targets, is completely original. (p 143, fig C)

TARGET SKILL
USA, ABT, 1925 (42x24x64cm). The moving target is in fact a big steel ball, 1cm in diameter, which appears at any one of five holes at the back of the machine. The player has just 45 seconds to shoot little steel balls, accompanied by a machine-gun noise. The score appears progressively on the front panel. (p 143, fig E)

77 L'ECLAIR (LIGHTNING)
France, Loubet, 1930 (55x26x27cm). Louis Loubet (1895 - 1979) started his apprenticeship with manufacturer Baptiste Chapsal at the age of 11 and, four years later, built his first machine. This was the first of a stream of roulettes, shooting galleries and football machines. After the 1937 ban in France, he manufactured coin-in-the-slot radios for hospitals and hotels, followed by the first parking meters at Orly Airport.

78 LE RAPID (QUICK FIRE)
France, possibly Loubet, circa 1925 (56x30x43cm). This is almost identical to the previous machine, still with automatic payment.

77 78

79 SANKT HUBERTUS SCHIESS AUTOMAT

Germany, Lochman, 1906 (53x39x25cm). Boar hunting. When the trigger is squeezed a fairly complicated mechanism suddenly shoots a long iron rod out of the barrel. There is an automatic pay-out if your aim is good.

80 ELECTRA

Germany, Electra, circa 1898 (68x59x29cm). A beautiful machine, complete with instructions on an enamelled plate. The coin is put into a slot in the gun and when the trigger is squeezed the coin itself is fired. In order to win the coin has to go into a slot exactly in the centre of the target. Automatic pay-out. The ebony cabinet-work is inlaid.

81 ELECTRA

Germany, Electra, circa 1899 (64x55x22cm). This is the same system as the 1898 model but with a different case. The instructions are now printed on the bevelled glass.

79

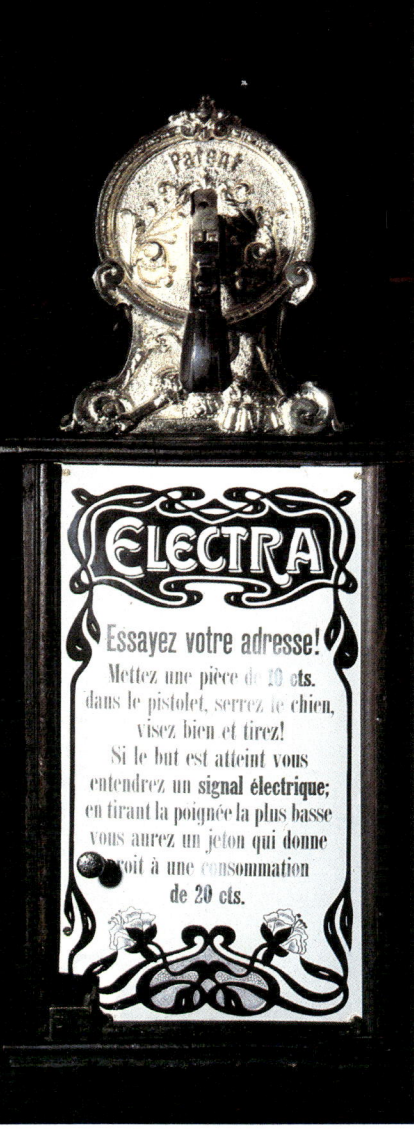

80

81

82 LA CHASSE (THE RABBIT SHOOT)

France, Le Dentu, circa 1910 (68x46x20cm). Although this type of game is usually known as *The Rabbit Shoot*, this machine was called *The Hunt* in the manufacturer's original catalogue. The rabbit is fixed to a big cogged iron wheel which turns when the money is put in and the heart is on an extra-long cog. When the trigger is squeezed, the wheel stops immediately due to the action of a rod. The pay-out is made only when the rod stops the longest cog and at the same time the rabbit gives a little cry caused by bellows in the mechanism. Automatic pay-out.

83 LA CHASSE A COURRE (THE HUNT)

France, Miquel (Foresty), 1937 (173x52x41cm). A superb machine 1.70m high. Put in the coin and turn the handle on the right. The horseman with his hunting horn follows the hounds hunting the stag. The player doesn't have to fire straight away: he can let the hunt pass until he is ready. Then he has to aim for the stag's heart and squeeze the trigger. If his aim is good, the stag gives a wild cry (as the instructions say), and the winnings drop down into the cup for collection.

Triple Reel Slot Machines

For most people coin operated machines conjure up the idea of one arm bandits which are the best known, most common and most evocative type of coin freed device.

For the vast bulk of its history the 3 reeler has been considered by western nations as an illegal gaming device. Yet for upwards of half a century they have been in common use in all the major urban centres. In legitimate areas, like the modern day Las Vegas, they can be encountered in their thousands. All existing to feed that mythical, magical hope of sudden fabulous fortune.

The documentary evidence for the invention of the 3 reel automatic payout gambling machine dates back to 1905/6 - the work of a Bavarian immigrant to the United States, Charles Fey. Earlier claims have yet to be substantiated. Although Fey was not aware of it at the time, he instinctively knew more about human nature than most psychologists. He realised that for the gambler the actual act of winning is only of subsidiary importance. There is as much pleasure, if not more, in loosing as there is in winning. Giving himself up to the whims of chance is the ultimate thrill.

The fact therfore that of 8,000 possible combinations on most 3 reelers made, only 12 are winners is of little relevance. More important are the 'just missed' combinations of potential winners. The addition of the jackpot in the late 1920s with its ever enhanced array of virtually unobtainable coins merely acted as an additional spur to the players' masochistic box of delights.

VICTORIA JACKPOT
USA, Jennings, 1931 (60x39x39cm). Fine modern decoration with light ray motif. (p 144, fig D)

WA-WO-NA
USA, Caille Co, circa 1910 (41x24x27cm). (p 144, fig 6). The American Indian crosses were removed at the time of the liberation of France in 1945 to avoid reprisals resulting from their resemblance to the Nazi swastika.

REGULAR OK MINT VENDER
USA, Mills 1926 (62x41x38cm). To get around the laws the owner had a notice printed which carried details of the most unlikely winnings - for example against two cherries and a a bell he put 'Tuck into a bowl of cherries'. (p 145, fig C)

F OK VENDER
USA, Mills, 1928 (65x41x41cm). This is a vivid example from the prohibition era of what a police sledge-hammer can do to a machine. The front has been split open and the cylinders bent out of shape so that the machine is unusable. The mark made by the blow is clearly visible beneath the cylinders. (p 144, fig F)

COMET BELL
USA, Pace, 1932 (65x41x41cm). Classic, very robust model (p 145, fig E)

VICTORIA PEACOCK
USA, Jennings, 1932 (62x40x40cm). The designer has used peacocks to attract his customers. (p 144, fig C)

84 PARIS COURSES (PARIS RACES)
France, Bussoz, 1911 (77x48x21cm). A forerunner of the 3 slot. One of Bussoz' finest machines. You back the colour of one of three horses which go round on three parallel tracks against a highly ornate, colourful racecourse. The mechanism is based upon the three reel principle.

85 ROULETTE VISIBLE
France. Bussoz, 1920 (75x62x21cm). Pierre Bussoz, the biggest French manufacturer, was ahead of his time when he invented his first automatic machine in 1892. He also conceived the idea of this machine which is quite different in that it has three horizontal reels.

84

85

86 ROLL OUT THE BARREL
England, Original Machine Manufacturers, 1940 (47x40x24cm).

87 ROL A TOP
USA, Watling, 1935 (67x41x38cm). Here is a real classic, one of the most sought after of the three reel fruit machines. It is equipped with two jack-pots and a gold award which paid out gold dollars.

88 TIERCE AND BELOTE
France, Martinache, 1935 (44x40x27cm). Although this machine has three reels, there is no jack-pot. The name refers to the popular French card game Belote, invented at the beginning of the 20th Century by Belot.

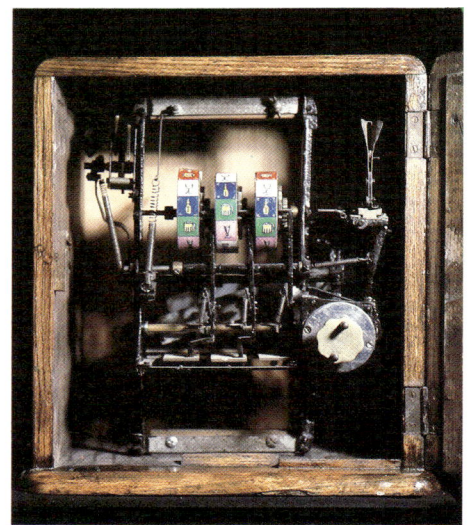

86

87

88

89 REGULAR OK MINT VENDER
USA, Mills 1926 (62x41x38cm). The use of the word regular here is to reassure the customer that he will get a fair deal from the machine.

90 OMEGA
Germany, Tura, circa 1926 (65x41x31cm). There is no lever at the side of this very old model. It has been replaced by a small handle on the front.

91 F OK VENDER
USA, Mills, 1928 (65x41x41cm). Instead of a jackpot on this model there are four columns which distribute sweets.

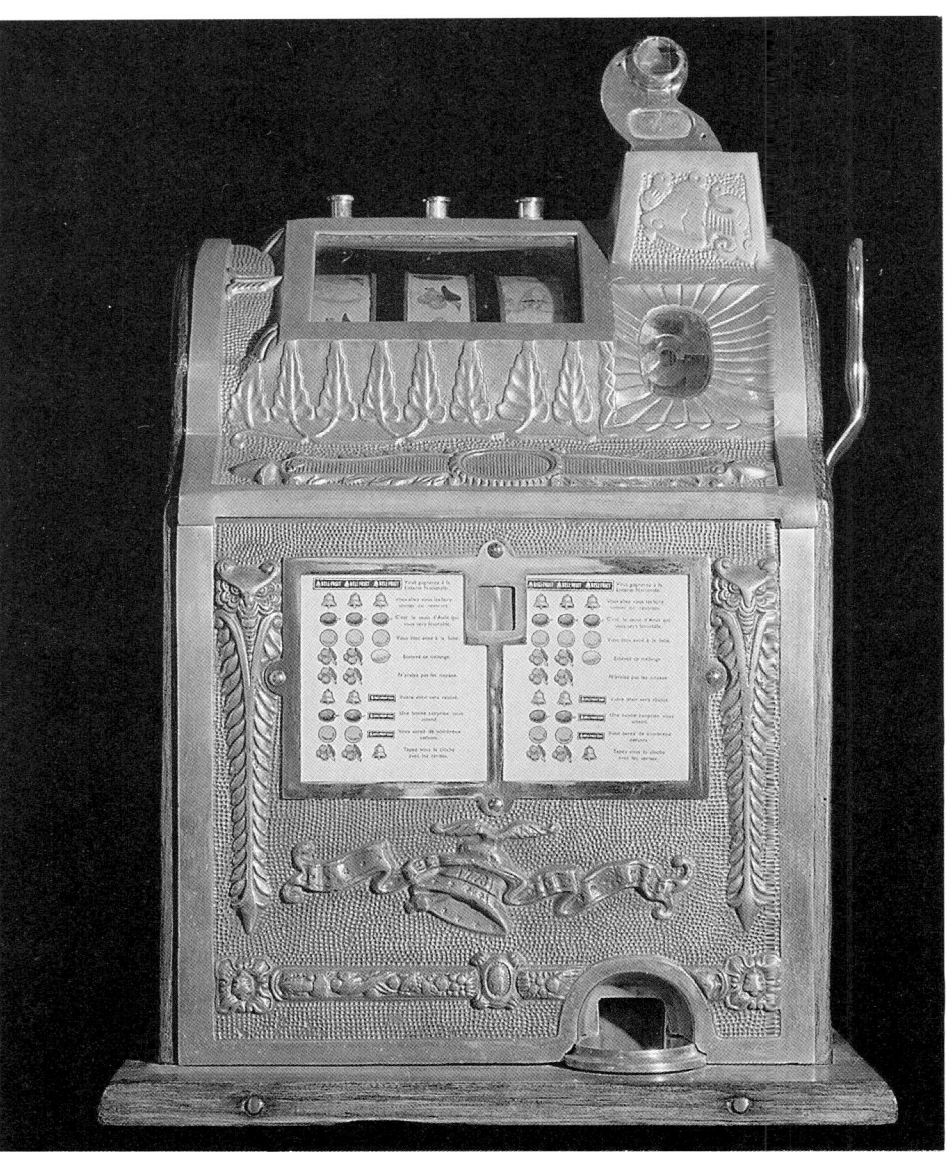

89

90

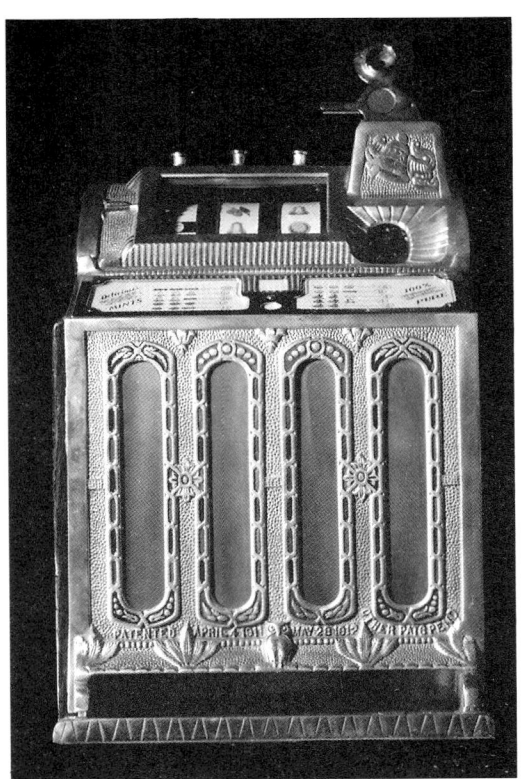

91

92 EXECUTIVE ELECTROVENDER

USA, Jennings, 1931 (78x40x41cm). When the Jennings company created this revolutionary model, the arm at the side was replaced by an electric button. Later however, to please the players who mourned the old system, the electrics were retained and the normal arm was reinstated. A rarely seen model which proved unpopular in use.

93 WA-WO-NA

USA, Caille, circa 1910 (41x24x27cm). This three reel model is rarely seen. The American Indian swastika crosses on the front are of particular note as only four other examples are known - compare the machine of the same name which is mentioned on page 78. The swastika cross with the head of an Indian was the emblem of the American Lafayette Division sent to Europe at the beginning of World War I.

92

93

94 DOMINO

France, Bignell, 1921 (60x43x20cm). The French name for the machine, Le Juge de Paix, is derived from a popular game commonly played in French cafes at the beginning of the century and is nothing to do with dispensing justice. The automatic magazine of December 1926 says on page 44 that R.C. Bignell was the inventor of this superb three reel, automatic machine. When the coin is put in and the knob turned, the gentleman rattles the dice box and the three reels, which look like dice, spin round. If they stop at a winning combination, as laid down in the rules of the game, the bar owner automatically raises his glass and the winning token appears in the cup. This is one of the very few European models distributed (by the Domino company) in the USA.

95 DUTCH BOY
   USA, Jennings, 1930 (68x39x36cm). A curiously childish decoration of gnomes or sprites.

96 SIMONIA
   This is a European revamp of a Mills Front O K Vender, circa 1929, designed to incorporate a jackpot device. Jackpots were in great vogue during the late 1920s and 30s.

97 BASE BALL
   USA, Mills, 1929 (62x41x41cm). Very interesting variant of the OK Vender.

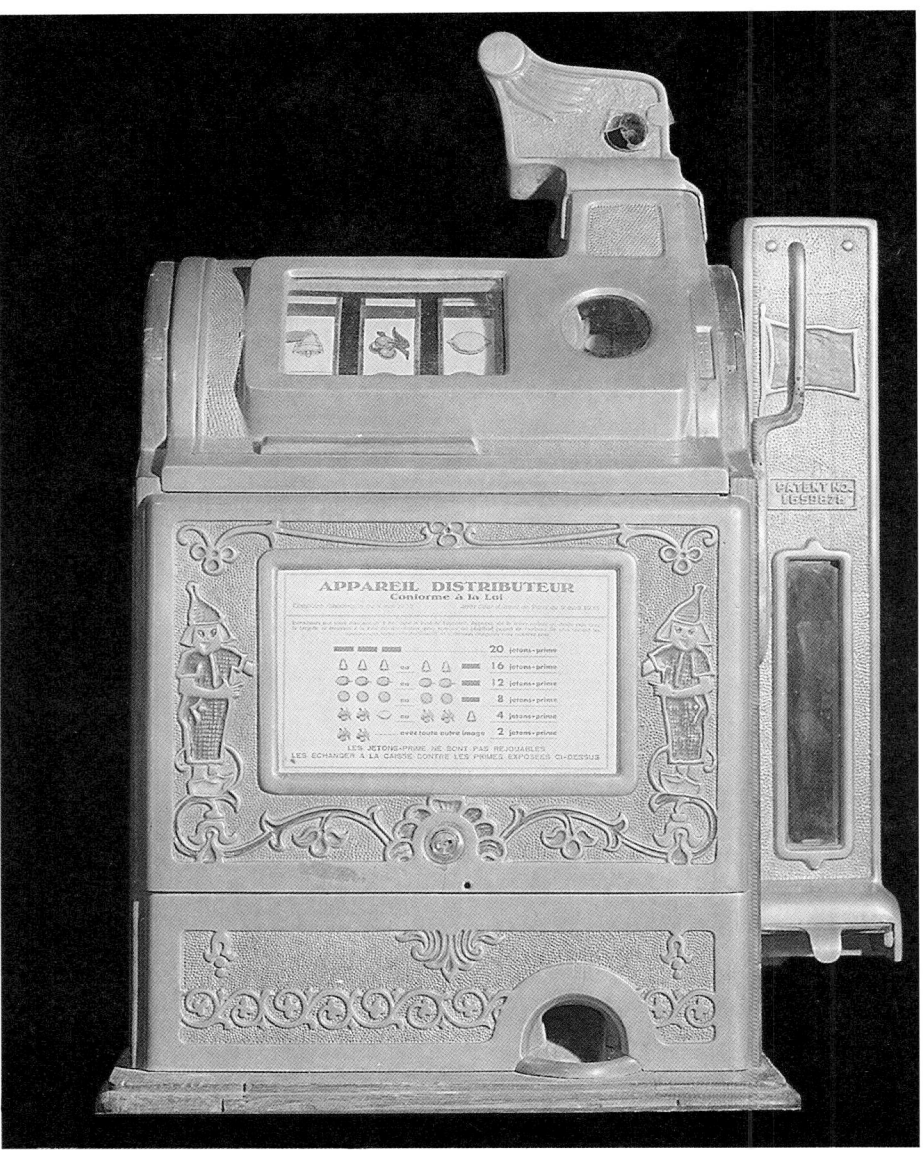
95

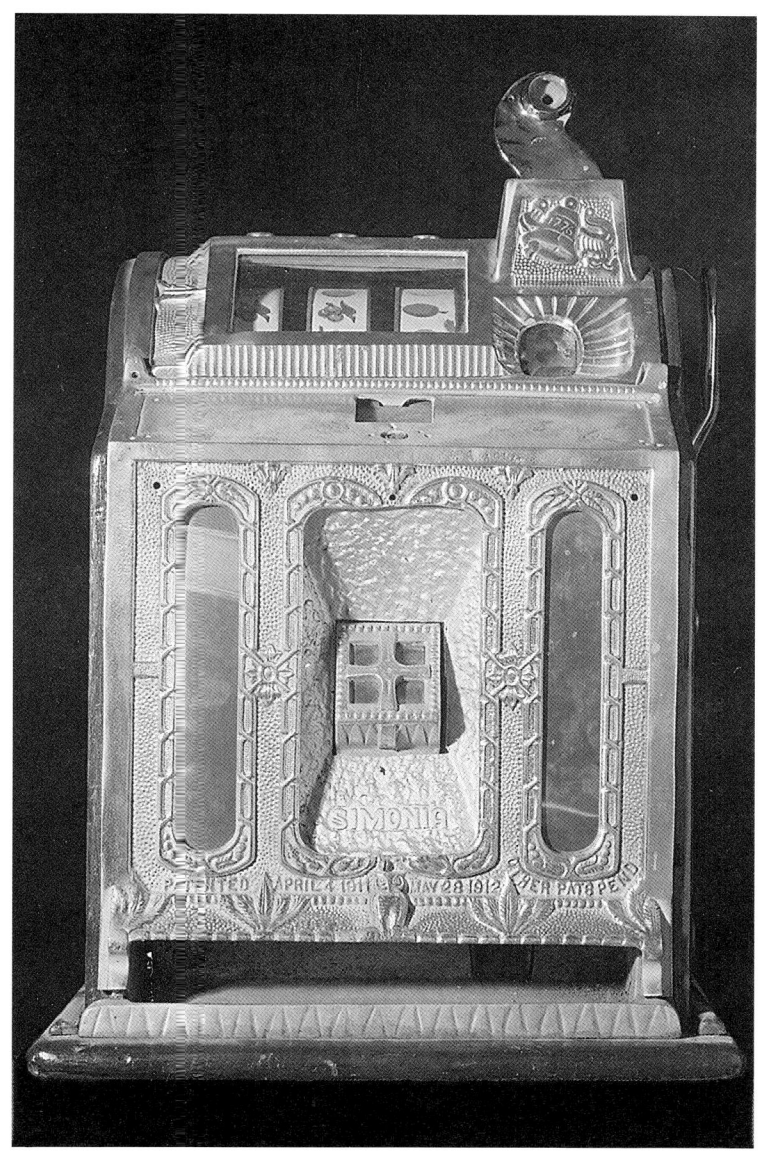

96

97

98 GRAND PRIZE
   USA, Caille Brothers, 1930 (60x37x30cm). This highly decorated machine is equipped with four reels instead of the usual three. This idea has been revived recently by manufacturers of electronic machines who often incorporate four or even five reels in their games.

99 TURA BELL
   Germany, Tura, 1933 (62x41x40cm). Tura was the only foreign manufacturer who managed to compete seriously with the Americans thanks to the help of a particularly dynamic and efficient French importer, Derouin. This strongly made machine rarely went wrong and was much prized by the players.

100 LES DOMINOS
   France, manufacturer unknown, circa 1915 (46x29x20cm). The only known example of this astonishing three reel machine.

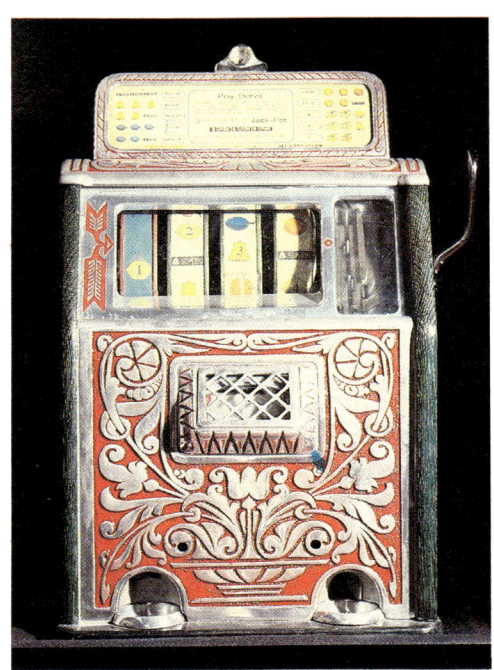

98

99   100

101 SKYSCRAPER
   USA, Mills, 1932 (64x41x37cm). This model is not as common as other Mills 3 reelers.

102 CONFECTION
   USA, Superior Confection Co, 1932 (54x31x36cm). A little known model by a little-known maker. There are two alternating jack-pots and a gold award with a gold dollar prize.

103 DOUGH BOY
   USA, Caille Co, 1935 (58x40x38cm). Sculpted in the purest Art Deco style.

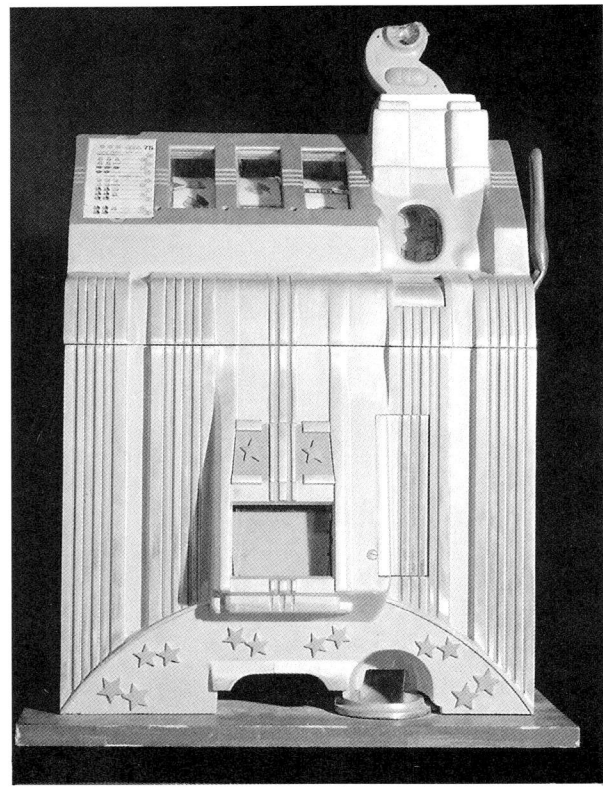

101

102

103

104 BLUE WAR EAGLE
   USA, Watling, 1933 (52x39x37cm). Watling, one of the oldest American firms, produced few models. However they all had the characteristic sound of the mechanism in common. It could not be matched and was, according to popular opinion, immediately recognisable by the players.

105 SILENT WAR EAGLE
   USA, Mills, 1931 (65x40x38cm). The first machine with a silent mechanism. At this period manufacturers were trying to find a way to reduce the noise but now with the advent of the silent electronic machines they are trying to add it. This example is beautifully decorated with a stylised eagle.

104

105

106 LITTLE DUKE
USA, Jennings, 1931 (55x33x21cm). This machine was the brain child of an Englishman, R C Bignell, the French importer of Jennings products. Its fame is due to its originality, the usual three reels having been replaced by concentric discs and the fruit symbols by stars. It was called *Little Duke* to join another model, *the Duchess*, in the Royal Family range launched by Jennings.

107 DUCHESS
USA, Jennings, 1930 (53x36x38cm). One of the Royal Family range detailed above.

106

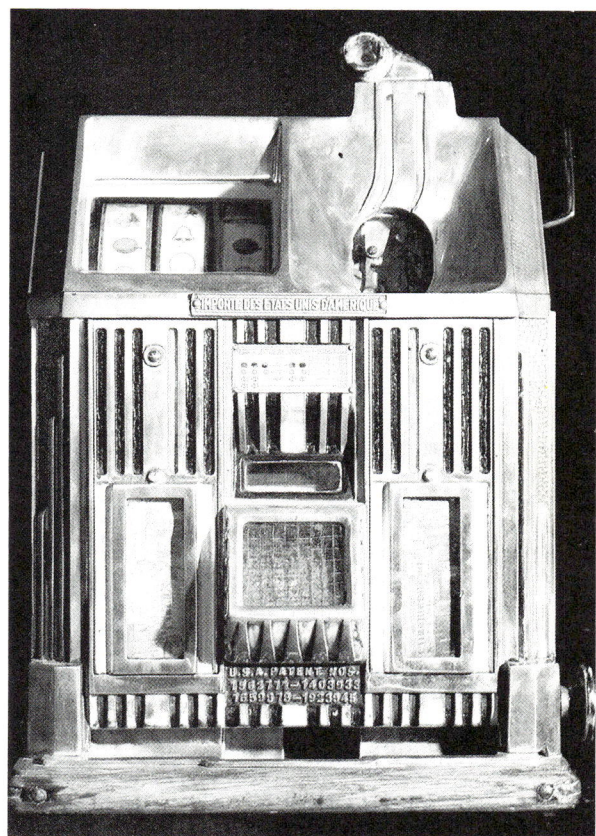

107

108 BONUS BELL
USA, Mills, 1937 (64x41x38cm). According to your score, the letters making up the word BONUS gradually appeared in the windows at the top of the machine. The complete word meant a high pay-out and so the player was motivated to continue playing.

109 BLACK BEAUTY
England, Tom Boland, 1956. (62x40x46cm). A revamp based on an earlier Mills mechanism.

110 BLACK CHERRY
USA, Mills, 1936 (65x40x38cm). Here the symbolic cherry has become the principal motif on the machine.

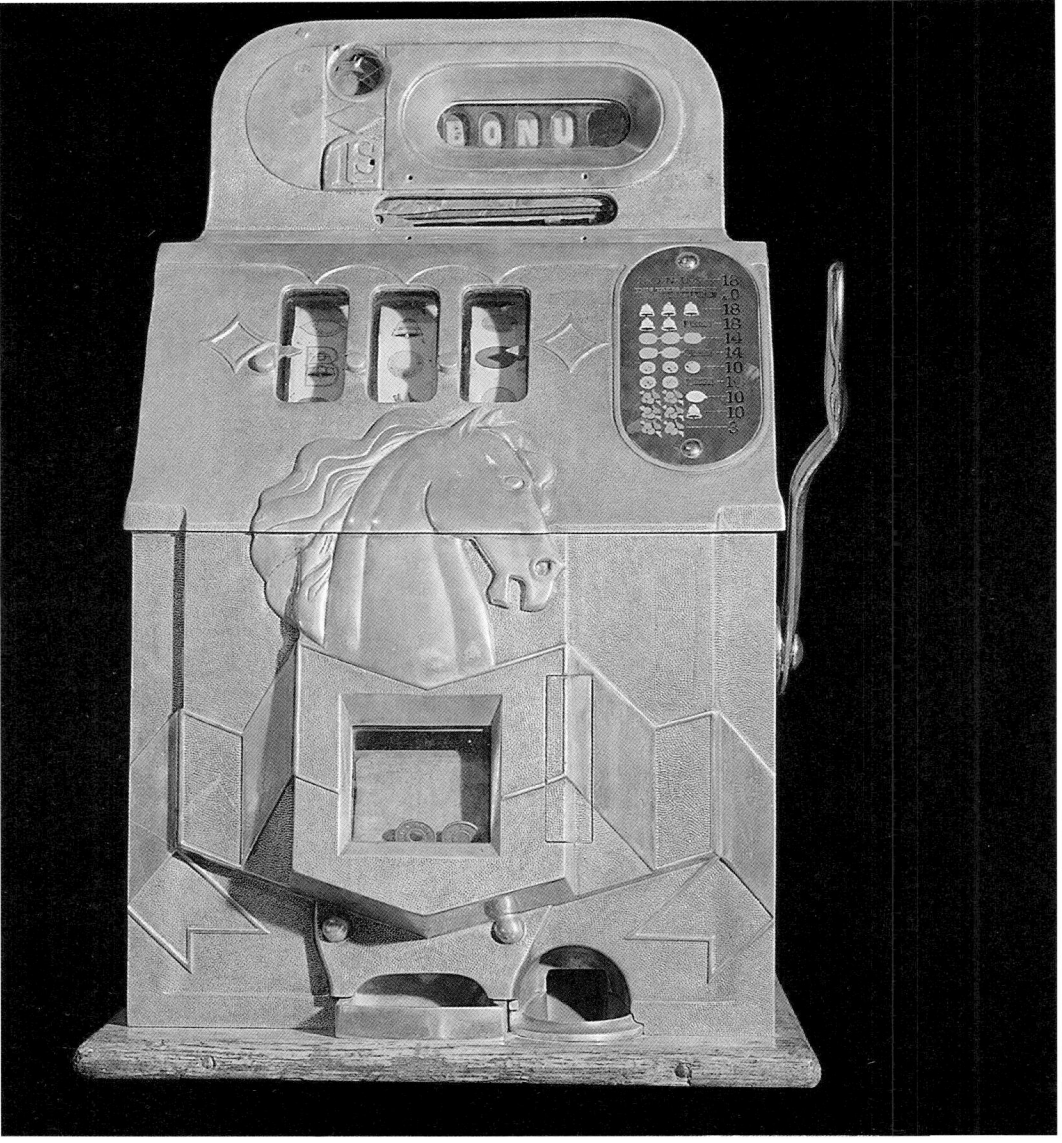

108

PACE BLANCHE COMET
USA, Pace, 1935 (60x41x41cm) (p 144, fig E).

CHIEF
USA, Jennings, 1936 (70x39x37cm). In the popular imagination the Indian was synonymous with adventure and so is a recurring decorative theme. This model has a double gold award. (p 145, fig A)

PACE ORANGE ALL STARS
USA, Pace, 1936 (p 145, fig B)

109

110

95

111 TOTALISATOR
England, Club Totalisator Co, circa 1933 (149x42x36cm). Uncommon, free standing model designed for use in clubs.

112 FAIR PLAY
England, Tom Boland, circa 1948 (63x36x38cm). A revamp based upon an earlier Mills mechanism. The name may have been chosen to reassure the players since many owners adjusted the machines in their favour.

GREY FRONT
USA, Mills, 1933 (74x36x35cm). Presented at the Chicago World Fair in 1933, this machine was also known in the USA as *World's Fair*, *Century* or *Extraordinary* and in France as *Cathedral* (p 145, fig D).

111

112

Trade Stimulators

The distinction between gambling machines and trade stimulators is based upon the presence, or absence, of an automatic pay out. Trade stimulators were generally, though not invariably, smaller and their function was seen as amusement rather than gambling. However they are usually grouped with gambling machines because inserting a coin brings an automatic response. In fact nearly all the distributors and cafe owners paid out winnings in cash under the very noses of the police who were trying to enforce the law. It was easy to do because the machines were within reach on the counter where the owner could keep an eye on the results without even moving. To prosecute, the police had to catch them in the act which was almost impossible. The two products were so alike that the authorities were confused and the gamblers were still amply catered for.

ZANZ
France, Joray, circa 1930(height 8cm,diameter 21cm). A 421 counter game with slot. The small lever at the side turns the roulette and the three balls spin round and settle into position. You get them back to the centre for the next game by pressing the little buttons. Same rules as for 421.(p 146, fig E)

PUNCH BOARD MACHINE
France, manufacturer unknown, circa 1930 (26x28x25cm). (p 146, fig B)

STELLA
France, Ludo, 1934 (52x40x15cm). In the 1930s the punch board games were very popular in America and Europe. Most makers produced their model either in the form of a board or a box with numbered holes to be pierced using the punch provided. Depending on the colour of the ball, the players were entitled to goods. This fine model looks rather like an old fashioned wireless. (p 146, fig C)

SIX COLOURS
France, Tolerie de Boulogne, 1936 (29x29x20cm). More than 4000 copies of the second model from this manufacturer were made. (p 141, fig D)

113

113 LOTERIE ROYALE
France, 1816 (diameter 56cm). One cannot speak about money games without mentioning the lotteries and lottery wheels that have been legal in France since 1539! This one in solid wood is decorated with fleurs de lys and dates from the First Restoration (1816) just after Napoleon's fall from power. It was probably made by a particularly talented showman and then became part of his stock-in-trade at fairs and markets.

114 FAIREST WHEEL
USA, Fairest Wheel Co, 1895 (44x31x23cm). The wheel was turned by placing a bronze ten cent coin into one of the slots at the top of the wheel. This machine was renowned for never breaking down.

115 DICETTE
USA, Jennings, circa 1930 (12x25x45cm), Curiously this roulette game is very rare.

114

115

116 L'ETONNANT
France, Grasset, 1898 (54x24x15cm). A simple but well thought out mechanism - simply put in a coin and the lottery wheels turn. If only the National Lottery could be as uncomplicated!

117 and 118 LOTERIES DE COMPTOIR (COUNTER MODELS)
France, 1850 - 1914 (33x20xdiameter 15cm). Although not equipped with money slots, these lotteries are the forerunners of the counter-top machines. They are fixed to a coloured metal base which in most cases holds a box of sulphur matches together with a grid to strike them on, thus allowing cafe customers who bought their cigars or cigarettes one at a time to light up at will. The wheels are hand-painted and glass-mounted and the themes are very varied - drinking scenes, courting scenes, the circus, industry, politics, mythology (including Bacchus of course!) and cycling. The 16 numbers go from 10 to 25,000 and a ball indicates the winning number. Despite an appeal on a popular French TV show no one can explain how this strange numbering scheme originated or the rules of the game. There must be between 100 and 150 examples still in existence. (p 144, Figs. A + B and p 146, fig A)

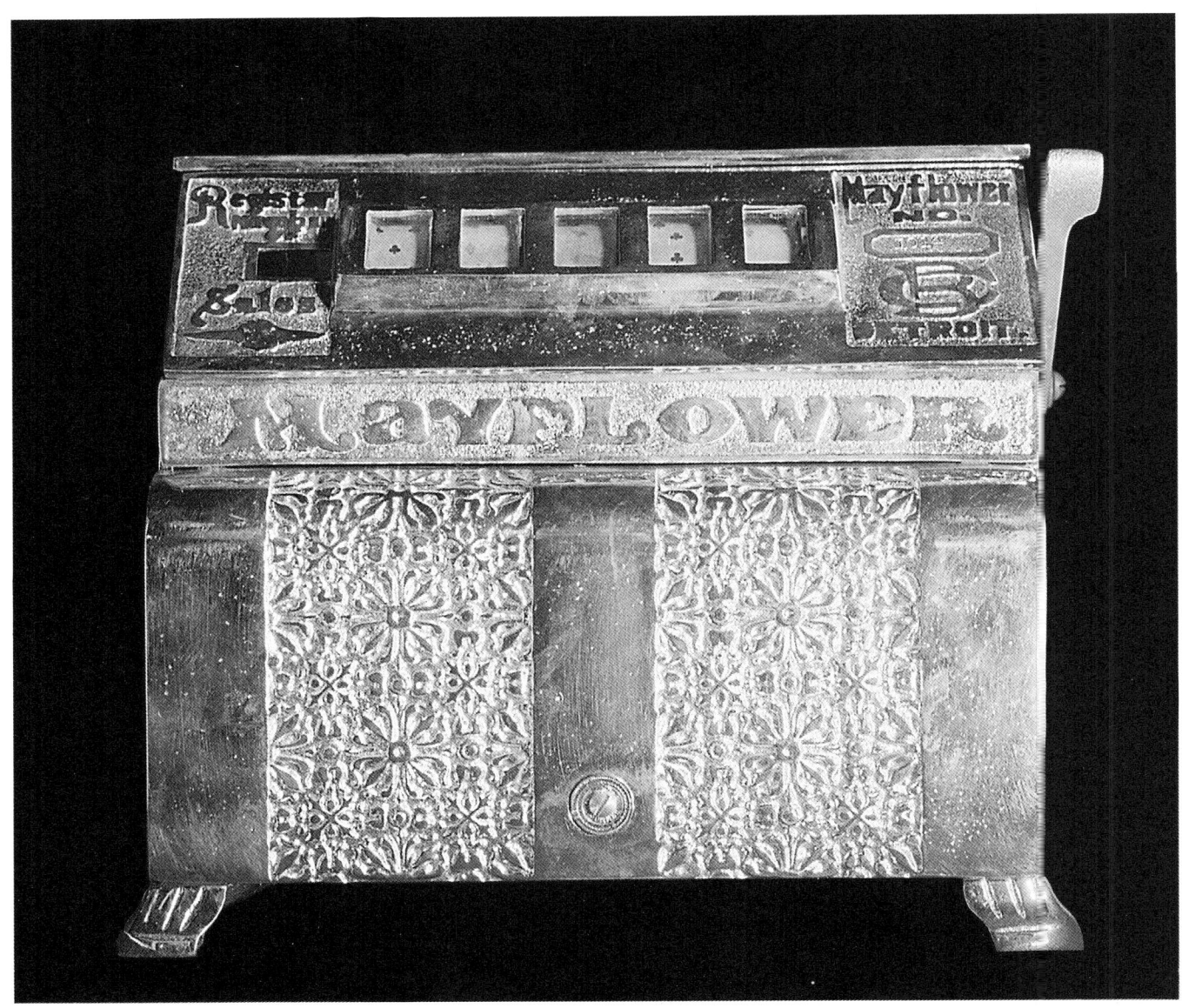

119

119 MAYFLOWER
USA, Caille, 1903 (23x27x18cm). This is an automatic poker game, named after the Pilgrim Fathers' ship.

120 SUPER POKER
France, manufacturer unknown, circa 1910 (35x23x20cm). The instructions were written on a very beautiful enamelled plate. The pressure of the coin pushed down on the disc holding the ivory dice so that it suddenly jumped and threw the dice. The same rules as for ace poker.

121 LITTLE PERFECTION
USA, Mills, 1910 (29x28x24cm). Poker, automatic style, was now within everyone's reach. Thanks to the ingenious mechanism, three cylinders turned one way and the two others in the opposite direction.

120

121

122 BOOP A DOOP
   USA, Pace, 1932 (43x23x18cm). This cheap counter game was very popular in the States during the Depression following the 1929 New York Stock Exchange crash. The balls are propelled into winning cups by the aid of small side lever.

123 NEGRO BALL
   France, manufacturer unknown, circa 1932 (37x23x18cm). This is a French revamp of Boop a Doop.

124 TOL BOUL
   France, Tolerie de Boulogne, 1930 (27x33x18cm). The big sphere is full of small balls of various colours. The handle on the left can be turned free of charge if the player thinks that he can improve his chances. Then, as soon as a coin is put in, a ball appears in the little window below the sphere, and you win according to the colour as shown on the list below. This model was to promote sales of Kremlina chocolate.

122

123

124

125 LE CAMELEON
France, Tolerie de Boulogne, 1935 (31x42x21cm). Counter top game whose winnings are paid out by the cafe owner, not by the machine. The win depends on the colour of the ball appearing when the 25cent coin is introduced.

126 LES BOXEURS
France, Ludo, 1932 (33x70x32cm). A game for two players, each with a handle to control one of the two boxers by means of pulleys and cables. If the boxer is in the right position, each punch of the lever raises, by a pneumatic system, the boxer's right arm. You have to knock-out your opponent's boxer within the 40 seconds regulated by an automatic timer. An exciting and extremely rare game.

125

127 TICKETTE
   USA, Mills, 1930 (23x78x24cm). After putting in your coin, choose a square on the grid and make a hole in it using the punch chained to the machine. This reveals a ball whose colour indicates how much has been won. There are two versions of this machine, one in wood the other in metal.

128 QUEEN TOP
   France, circa 1930 (19x33x27cm). An amazing counter-top machine with three horizontal discs. An arrow points to the winning combination. This includes the usual classic symbols such as oranges, cherries, plums, bells and some new shapes like suns, stars and green dots.

126

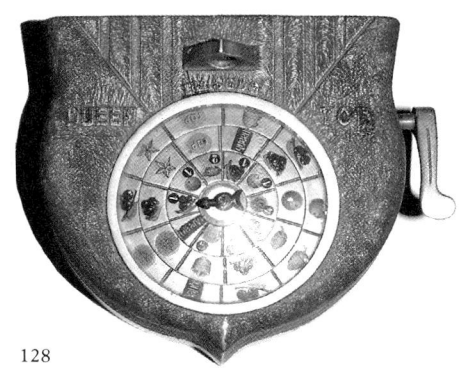

128

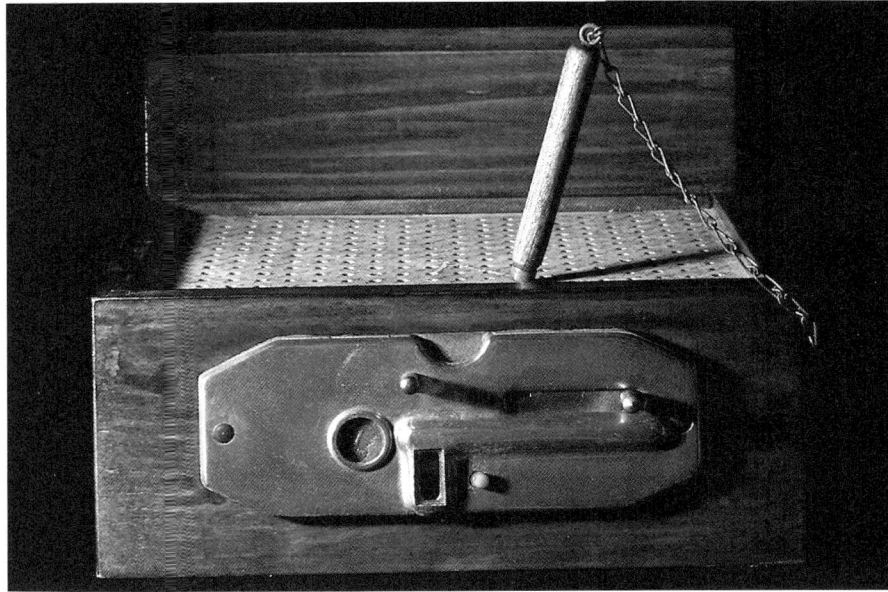

127

Scales and Strength Testers

Although they do not pay out money, these machines do belong to the classic slot machine family as they take money and have a mechanical system. They allow the player to show off his strength and were especially popular at fairs and amusement arcades.

SCALES
France, circa 1900 (205x42x58cm) (p 142, fig E)

SCALES
France, Chameroy, 1903 (211x44x60cm) (p 146, fig D)

SCALES
France, circa 1900 (210x45x57cm) (p 142, fig A)

DELIVER THE PUNCH
USA, Mills, 1904 (200x46x100cm). Automatic and suprisingly large punch-ball, 2 metres high and 120 kilos in weight! The bag is attached to a heavy spring by a chain and the tension increases when the player punches the bag. (p 142, fig C)

OLYMPIA PUNCHER
USA, Caille 1905 (158x47x65cm). "Hit me and I'll tell you how strong you are." No complicated instructions, no risk. (p 142, fig B)

LA FORCE DE LA MAIN (STRENGTH OF HAND)
France, Braesch, 1908 (40x27x16cm). Each year during their quiet season showmen would service and repaint their equipment. Some showed real talent and produced remarkable results. This little counter machine is a fine example of the genre.

129 BALANCE DE GARE (RAILWAY SCALES)
France, circa 1895 (210x48x55cm). This superb machine is a fine example of highly decorated cast iron.

129 (détail)

129

130 MUSCLE TESTER
   USA, Rosenfield, circa 1903 (162x36x58cm). To use this machine you try to force the two handles together.

131 SAMSON LIFTER
   USA, Caille, circa 1905 (160x24x58cm). The name encourages the player to emulate Samson's tremendous power. Lift the two handles, push upwards as far as you can.

132 L'ATHLETE COMPLET
   France, Barme, 1932 (221x40x52cm). Here the athlete can measure the strength of his wrist and arm. Gradually as he increases the pressure the lights on the dial illuminate the bridge in the picture. This machine has been disguised as Marius, a Marseille character, and even the indicator is a fish. The eyes light up as well.

130 (détail)

130

131

132

133 AJAX PUNCHER
USA, Caille, 1904 (223x50x65cm). This is a rare model. At 2.20m high it was very bulky and heavy, so the manufacturer replaced it with the easier to handle Olympia Puncher.

134 UNCLE SAM
USA, Caille circa 1908 (195x38x40cm). Uncle Sam was always popular with Americans who wanted to shake his hand. They could show their patriotism and measure the strength of their right hand at the same time thanks to the figure's articulated little finger. A bell rang if their strength reached the 300 level. However prospective collectors should beware as copies of this machine were manufactured in the late 1970s.

135 APOLLO
USA, Caille, circa 1908 (220x63x50cm). The player tested his strength in an arm wrestling match with Apollo by trying to force the figure's right arm (made of coloured iron) down as far as it would go. 2.20m high, this is one of the most spectacular and rare strength machines.

133   133 (détail)

134

135

Electric Shock Machines and Viewers

In the last two decades of the 19th century anything electrical was considered unusual and attracted the passer-by. Electricity was thought to have boundless powers: 'Electricity is Life' proclaimed one and all. As well as giving strength, energy, health, it was even believed to cure rheumatism. So what a godsend for the machine manufacturers always on the look out for another novelty. All it needed was two voltaic batteries or a small accumulator, an induction coil and last, but not least, the coin mechanism, and you were in business.

SIMPLEX
USA, Caille, circa 1902 (55x39x26cm). Note the elegance and simplicity of the design on this machine which is still being restored. (p 141, fig E)

L'ELECTRISEUR VERT (GREEN ELECTRIC SHOCKER)
France, Meyer, circa 1905 (54x40x13cm) (p 141, fig B)

L'ENERGIE
France, circa 1910 (76x39x13cm) (p 149, fig B)

ELECTRIC SHOCKER
France, Braesch, circa 1910 (47x37x20xm). (p 150, fig D)

L'ELECTRISEUR BARME (ELECTRIC SHOCKER)
France, Barme, circa 1930 (75x64x25cm). A light comes on at each stage reached by the player. (p 150, fig E)

136 LE PETIT MEYER
France, Meyer, circa 1920 (27x37x20cm).

137 LE FEU (FIRE)
France, manufacturer unknown, circa 1910 (58x37x16cm). The two handles shaped like hands are most unusual.

138 L'ORAGE (THE STORM)
France, Braesch, circa 1905 (53x40x12cm). The superb decoration speaks for itself.

139 LE COCHON ELECTRISEUR (ELECTRIC SHOCKER PIG)
France, Maurice & Molle, circa 1898 (81x41x27cm). A handsome model pig complete with a goodluck clover leaf on his collar. Put your coin in the neck, hold the knob with your left hand and slowly turn the handle on the right with the right hand. The object is to see if you can take the electric surge shown by the dial on his belly until the pig's eyes light up.

137

138

140

141

140 LE MOTOCINE
France, Martin, circa 1930 (80x47x16cm). The beginning of blue movies, a strip-tease for 25 centimes, and definitely not for children. The coin operates a mini-projector and a mini-screen using a 9mm loop film.

141 STEREOSCOPE AUTOMATIQUE
France, circa 1930 (45x33x31cm). For 1 franc you can see a three dimensional picture of ladies - bathing or just scantily dressed.

142 LE DIRIGEABLE (THE AIRSHIP)
Germany, Jentzsch and Meerz, circa 1929 (80x47x16cm). This wall mounted machine incorporates an electric shock device commonly used as a legal ploy to circumvent anti-gambling laws. The game features the R100 airship built in the UK in 1929.

142

Fortune Tellers

Since the beginning of time men have longed to know their future, so it is hardly surprising that manufacturers exploited this deep desire. The first machine by Pierre Bussoz predicted the future, but very few of the early models exist.

L'ORACLE
France, Bussoz, 1920 (75x62x20cm). (p 141, fig C)

PROFIT SHARING REGISTER
USA, Mills, circa 1900 (42x24x12cm). Designed to sit on, and work in conjunction with, a cash register, this machine gave the customer a free chance to win extra merchandise. (p 149, fig A)

ST DUNSTAN'S HOROSCOPE
England, manufacturer unknown circa 1905 (42x45x12cm). This is in the uncommon form of a church offertory box. Nothing was sacred to the machine manufacturers as can be seen in one of their French brochures; 'In all the countries of the world, thousands of automatic machines are employed to fund the Red Cross, Schools, Hospitals, Orphanages, Churches, The Poor Fund, Pensions and Charities.' (p 149, fig C)

LA MARGEURITE (THE DAISY)
France, Barme, 1926 (75x66x14cm) (p 142, fig F)

L'AVENIR (THE FUTURE)
France, Bonzini & Sopransi, circa 1937 (69x44x20cm). The roulette has been modified by an operator to give an automatic reading of the lines on your palm. (p 149, fig E)

THE ANSWERITE
England, Barwicks Automatics, circa 1944 (69x49x17cm) (p 141, fig A)

143 L'EGYPTIEN
France, circa 1925 (45x38x22cm). This Egyptian is a real expert, giving horoscopes according to age and sex.

144 POST OFFICE
England, circa 1898 (74x32x25cm). This extraordinary machine sold horoscopes. Its English pillar-box shape is very rare.

143

144

145 MISS TYKA
France, Barme, 1925 (75x66x14cm)

146 CE QUE DISENT VOS YEUX
(IT'S IN YOUR EYES)
France, Barme, 1925 (64x51x20cm). There is a choice of four colours, but if you have green eyes or are an albino, you are out of luck! There are very few of these machines still in existence.

145

146

Vending Machines

In France, in 1936, a very interesting state of affairs existed. There were two competing trade federations, the Automatic Machine Federation and The Automatic Confectionery Vendors Association. The first grouped together distributors, owners, traders, importers, manufacturers, in fact anyone and everyone connected with coin-operated slot machines except for 3 reelers. The second, despite its inoffensive sounding name, concerned itself solely with 3 reel machines. However, one must not be misled by this legal subtlety: vending machines only gave goods, not money or tokens for drinks or encashment. Pretty soon manufacturers realised they could sell many more products than previously by using the machines to increase their outlets. Generally speaking, with a few exceptions, these machines had fairly simple mechanisms. The important element was their appearance which had to attract and persuade the customer in the absence of a salesman - thus the shape and decoration were usually well researched. Some are masterpieces of industrial art.

One could also include horoscope and electric-shock machines in this category but, as is more usual, they have already been dealt with separately in the previous two chapters.

FREDS
USA, National, 1897 (13x8x10cm). This tiny wall mounted machine distributes matches, one at a time. It is a pity that it has no coin-slot mechanism. (p 150, fig F)

CASH REGISTER
USA, National, circa 1890 (48x60x39cm). It is not a true slot machine but it was, after all, essential for giving change. (p 155, fig D)

HARVARD STAMPER
USA, Harvard Automatic Machine Co, 1923 (151x52x52cm). This engraving machine is being restored. Your coin gave you 25 letters or numbers stamped in relief on a metal strip to keep as a souvenir. (p 153, fig A)

LE CYCLONE
France, circa 1930 (38x34x30cm). A nickel plated version of the Cyclone razor blade vending machine. (p 149, fig D)

TAXIBRIQUET
France, Taxibriquet, 1928 (23x13x8cm). A small automatic lighter fuel machine. (p 153, fig B)

DISTRIBUTEUR D'ESSENCE (PETROL VENDER)
France, Appareils Controleurs, circa 1930 (38x17x14cm) (p 150, fig B)

SWEET VENDER
Circa 1930 (48x20x15cm) (p 150, fig C)

AUTOMATIC BAR
Manufacturer unknown, circa 1920 (240x137x74cm). 2m high and 2.5m wide, this machine weighs 140 kilos and gave a choice of 20 drinks. Being restored. (p 153, fig E)

STAMPS
USA, Shipman Mfg, circa 1938 (41x20x15cm). Has an enamelled metal front. (p 150, fig A)

147 LE PECHEUR (THE FISHERMAN)
France, JAF, 1934 (182x60x55cm). This is the only known automatic crane mechanism in the form of a fisherman. The left hand knob moves him from left to right, or vice versa, while the right hand one enables him to catch the fish and put it straight into the hole on the right. The fish can then be retrieved from the drawer beneath the knobs.

148 POULE AUTOMATIQUE (AUTOMATIC HEN)
Germany, Richard Reichert, circa 1930 (64x54x28cm). Reichert was based at Leipzig, the capital of the German automatic industry.

147

148

149 JOHN BULL

England, Jofeh, circa 1903 (83x52x23cm). This cigar and cigarette machine was made by John Jofeh, the important English pioneer who died in 1925. Put in a penny, depress the lever at the front, let go suddenly and the penny is thrown up, either into the top cup which wins a cigar, or into the easier middle cup which wins you a cigarette. The cigar comes down and through the slot on the left side and the cigarette on the right. Everybody wins because the coin goes back to the beginning if it does not land in a cup, and is played time and time again, until it does.

150 POST CARD VENDER

Germany, circa 1900 (144x32x32cm). The post card was invented by an Austrian in 1870. Introduced into France in 1872, they became really popular at the time of the 1889 Universal Exhibition in Paris - in 1900 more than a thousand million cards were printed in Germany, 800 million in America and 600 million in France. By 1911 Mills' catalogue was already showing 12 working post card machines. They were huge and very few are to be found now. Possibly they went for scrap. This German version is a superb example of the influence of Art Nouveau on the machine. It sold cards giving assignations! (the text is simulated hand-writing)

149

150

151 LE CYCLONE
France, circa 1930 (40x33x33cm). Manufacturers found ways to make vending machines for everything possible, perfumes, cigars and cigarettes, petrol, post cards and even, as here, razor blades. Compare the version shown in fig.D on page 149.

152 BALL GUM VENDER
USA, Colombus, circa 1935 (height 35, diameter 22cm). A beautiful copper vending machine in the shape of a diver's helmet.

153 MALAUSSENA
USA, made for export to France, circa 1912 (48x22x20cm). The design is based upon the Little Perfection peanut vender.

154 VAPOLUX
France, manufacturer unknown, circa 1930 (160x43x33cm). Automatic scent-spray in pure Art Deco style. It offered a choice of four perfumes - amber, chypre, lilac and oreganum - and the spray was obtained by turning handle on the right

151

152

154

127

155

156

128

155 POULE PONDEUSE AUTOMATIQUE (AUTOMATIC LAYING HEN)

France, Leoni, circa 1897 (54x54x37cm). As it engagingly states on the enamelled instruction plate, 'This hen clucks'. Put in the coin, pull the ring beneath the instructions and a metal egg containing sweetmeats appears in a hole on the right. Meanwhile, using small wood and paper bellows, the hen is clucking happily away.

156 L'ELEPHANT
Germany, HC, circa 1898 (80x55x27cm). This splendid painted metal elephant complete with howdah, the only one of its kind, sells little chocolate bars.

157 LIGHTER FUEL VENDER
France, Le Cosaque, circa 1937 (29x32x24cm).

157

158 PARKING METER
   USA, 1960 (33x11x11cm). Louis Loubet installed parking meters at the new Orly air terminal in 1960.

159 PLAYERS PLEASE
   England, 1928 (65x28x21cm). Cigarette vending machine advertising and dispensing Players Navy Cut cigarettes.

160 MATCHES
   USA, Mills, 1911 (38x28x24cm). 96% of men smoked so match vending machines were essential, according to Mills. A good example of marketing!

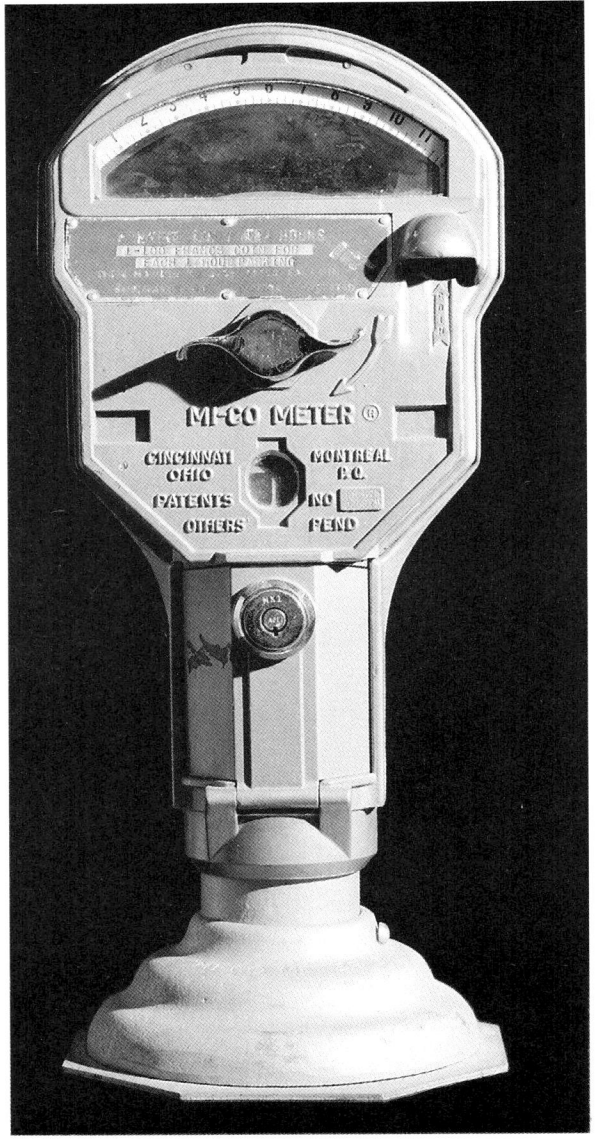

158

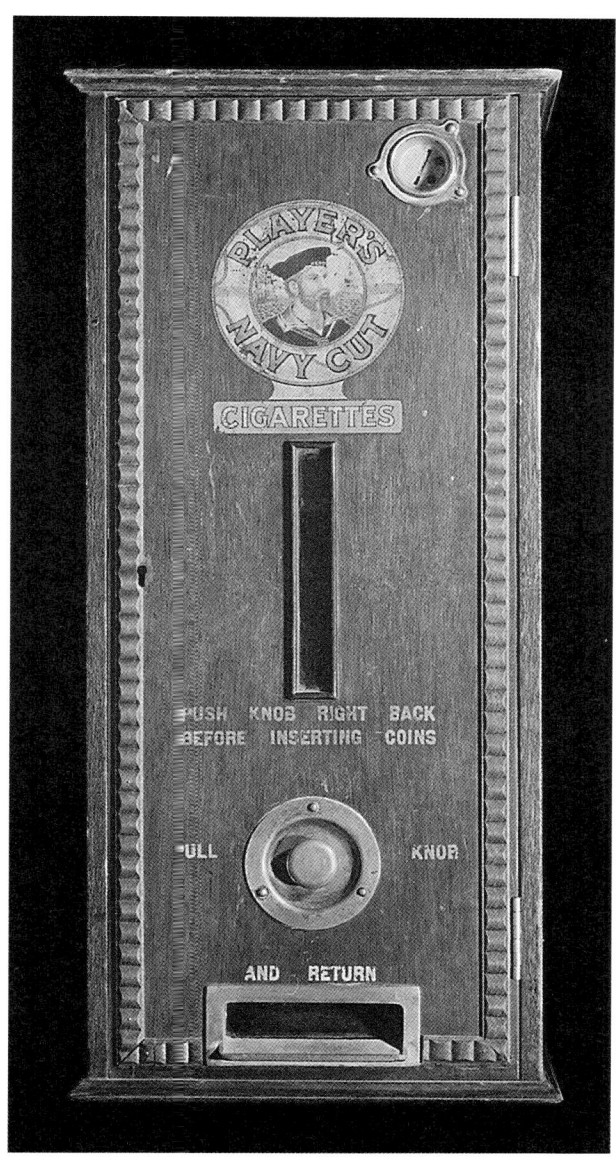

159

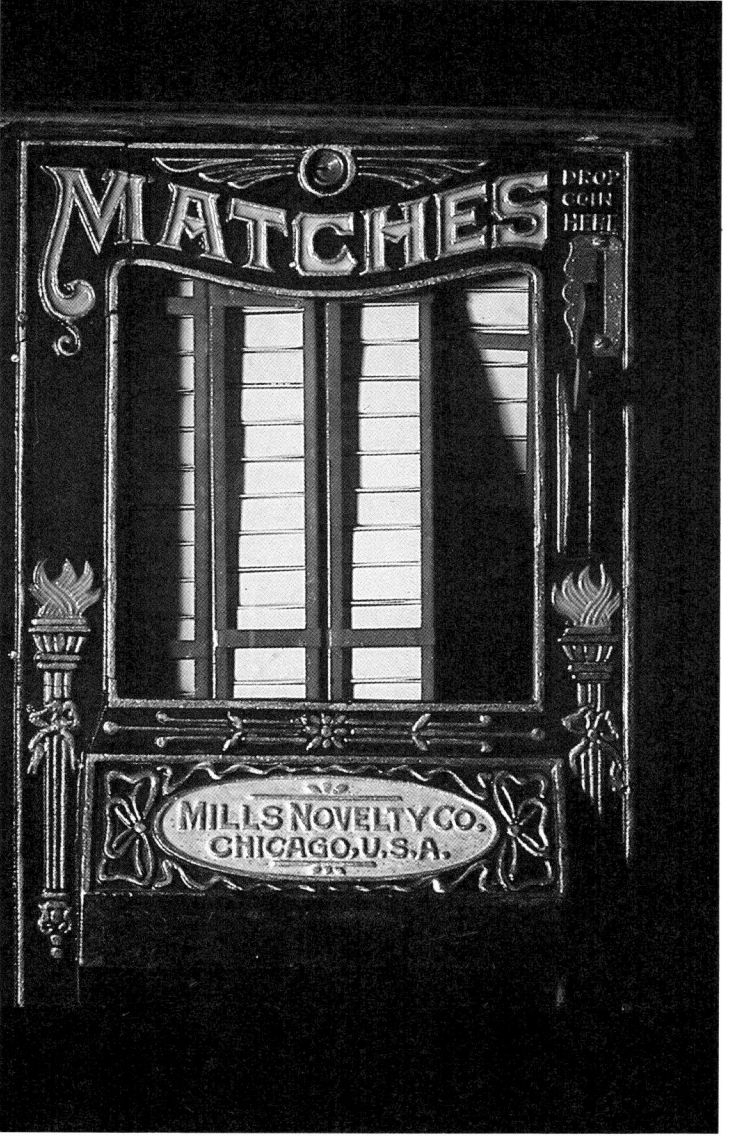

160

Pintables, Billiards and Bagatelle

In the Iliad Homer tells of the Greek warriors who, while laying seige to Troy, relieved the tedium by rolling pebbles into holes made in mounds of earth. After such a promising start it unfortunately took another two thousands years to produce the mechanical billiards machine as we know it now.

161 LA TOUR DE PARIS'
France, Bonzini and Sopransi, 1933 (93x41cm). The most beautiful and the most rare mechanical billiards was perfected by the American Rock Ola firm in 1933 and distributed under the name of Jigsaw. The Tower of Paris is its French counterpart. Each time a ball falls into a winning hole a picture appears. The point of this game is to put together a twenty picture puzzle representing the main sights of Paris such as the Eiffel Tower, Trocadero (replaced by the Chaillot Palace in 1937), the Arc de Triomphe, Opera and the Madeleine. Early machines had pins to deflect the balls, the bumper not coming into use until three years later.

162 ROTUOR
France, Rotuor Co, circa 1915 (35x55x53cm). The Rotuor has a spring-less mechanism for shooting the balls which are made of ivory and the board is slightly inclined. The mechanism is simple. Put in the coin, turn button number one to release the balls and then the second button to put one ball in position which is pushed by a wooden implement on the right. Since the rules of the game have been lost, it is assumed that white loses, green wins one, orange wins two, blue wins three and red wins four.

LE SKEE BALL
USA, Skee Ball Co, circa 1922 (29x100cm). The ball is delivered with some force, bounces off a kind of spring-board and lands in a target made up of concentric metal circles. Each circle has a hole which drops the ball into a numbered holder (from 50 to 100). (p 151, fig E)

161

162

133

FOOTBALL STAAR
France, Meunier, 1920 (107x92x49cm). This solid oak table for two players, worked by two handles, can be considered an ancestor of the popular game of table-football. Football's popularity inspired numerous automatic machines. This one was invented by a Belgian, G Staar and built by a Frenchman, R Meunier, in Orleans. Note the superb round glass top protected by metal strips. (p 152, fig D).

LE SATURNE
France, manufacturer unknown 1935 (102x47x47cm). The manufacturer explains that the game is so named because of its cratered planet-like appearance. The player is allowed to tilt the machine at will to get the ball into the middle hole indicated by an arrow. If he does, he wins a 50 or 75 centime token to buy a drink at the bar. (p 152, fig A)

LE LABYRINTHE ROUGE (RED MAZE)
France, 1931 (50x75cm). A surprising game that is quite the opposite of the classic mechanical billiard game. Here you have to prevent the ball falling into the holes. The lever lifts the red ball onto the board, and two decorative knobs guide it into the red hole. The winning token is found in the drawer. This is the only known example. (p 151, fig C)

RAILWAY
England, 1934 (80x44cm). Daval's American Chicago Express of 1934 inspired an English maker to use the same railway theme. The very small dimensions of this game make it particularly charming. It also has a free play hole. (p 152, fig C)

BILL HOP LUX
France, manufacturer unknown, circa 1933 (100x48cm). The decoration of this model is clearly influenced by avant-garde artists and is almost kinetic in style. The balls return to their places (numbered 100 to 1,000) at the lower end of the machine. (p 152, fig B)

LE PARCOURS AUTOMOBILE (CAR RACE)
France, Autoreflex, 1934 (97x129x65cm). The racing car does not move but the road, painted on a canvas roller, moves beneath it automatically. You have to avoid the obstacles and the counter keeps track of accidents, notably the number of run-over ducks. (p 151, fig B)

L'AUTOROUTE SPORTIVE (SPORTS CAR)
France, Autoreflex, 1937 (100x132x66cm). The same principle as above, but the steering wheel moves the car from side to side to keep to the 'rolling' road. There is a foot accelerator and a luminous screen. 46 years ahead of its time, this early car video game was invented by Billon, the founder of the Autoreflex company. (p 151, fig A)

LIGA
Germany, Tura, 1936 (116x59cm). The first dry battery electric pin table game was invented in 1933. It was not successful but many manufacturers saw its potential. This game is noteworthy because it was the first time that Tura - already well known in Europe for their fruit machines - had used electricity. The two footballers, each standing by their goal, automatically kick out as soon as the ball touches them. Obviously the results are unpredictable. It was also in 1936 that Bally, in the USA, invented the Bumper game with electrified sprung mushrooms to return the balls more forcefully. (p 152, fig E).

Juke Boxes

The term *juke-box* is fairly recent. Previously people talked about the automatic phonogram but it was not quite the same thing. However, it is interesting to note that one of the first machines to resemble the modern juke box used 78 rpm records and was invented in 1921 by the Frenchman, Pierre Bussoz. So it is only fair to give him a credit for his contribution. The same year the American Wurlitzer bought the patent from Bussoz.

AUTOPHONE
France, Daviet, circa 1930. Interesting automatic gramophone with two turntables. (p 151, fig D)

163 BUSSOPHONE

France, Bussoz, 1921 (160x90x70cm). An entirely automatic machine, the dial at the right is used to select the chosen record from the twenty available. You put in a 25 centime coin, turn the handle as far as it will go and the record, already on a metal frame, slides to a point just above the turntable which turns and rises. It comes into contact with the long-play needle and the music is heard through the box on top of the machine. The motor is not worked by a spring but by counterweights attached by fine strings. When the handle is turned, the weights rise and, in falling, drive the turntable. No electricity is used in this machine, one of six known examples, but everything operates simultaneously and automatically.

163

Illustrations of the Other Machines Mentioned in the Text

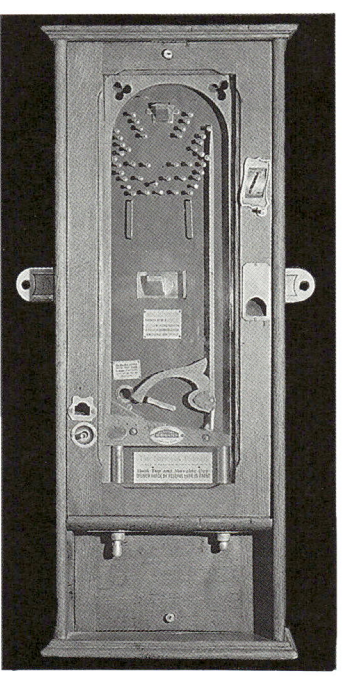
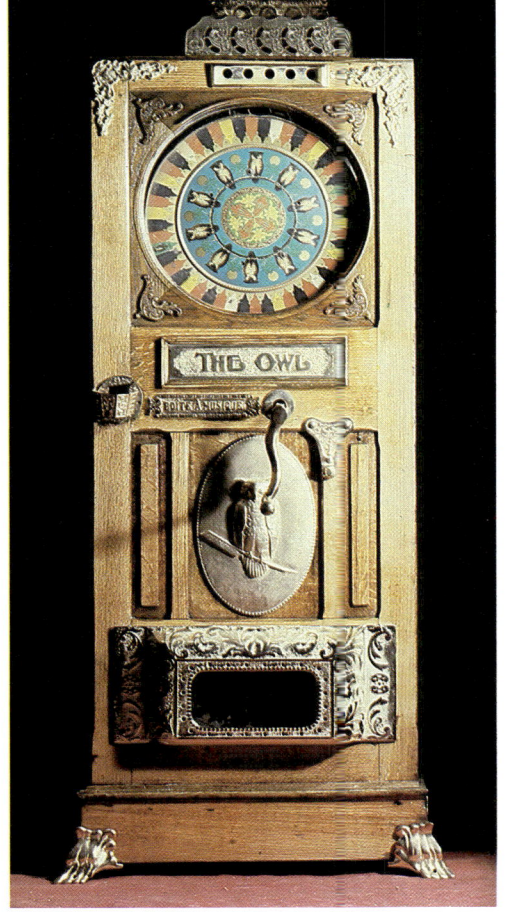

A
B C D

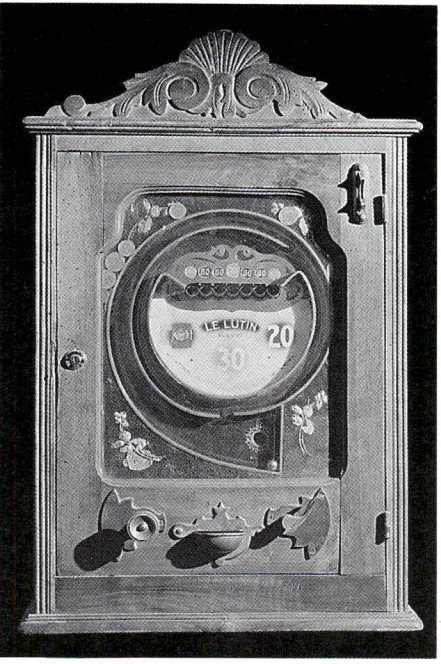

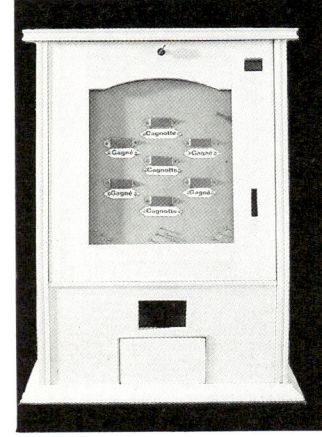

A	B	C
D	E	

140

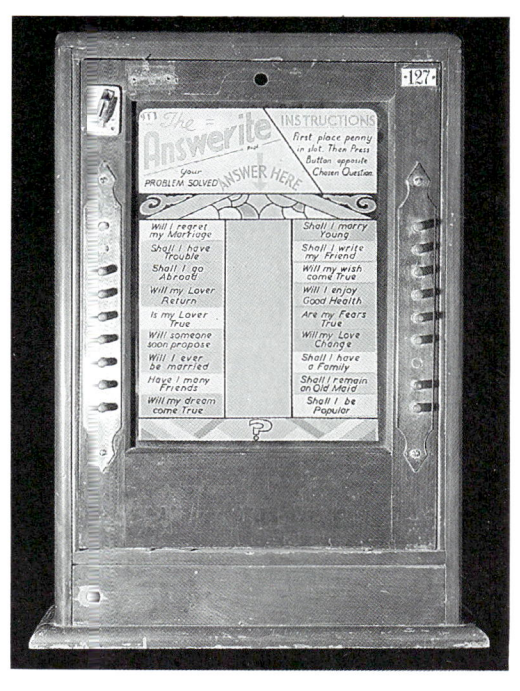

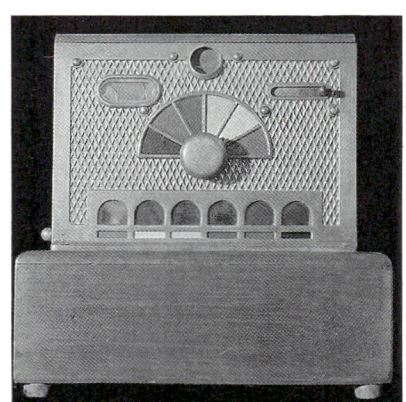

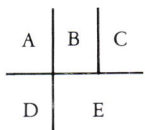

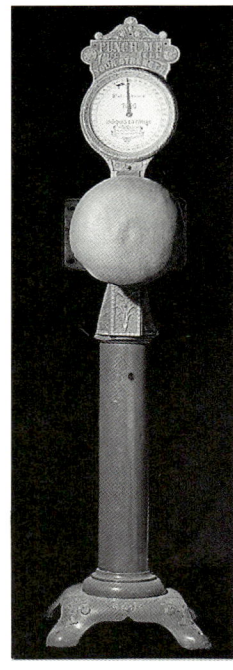

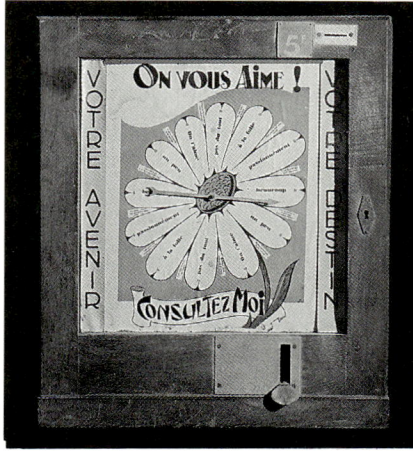

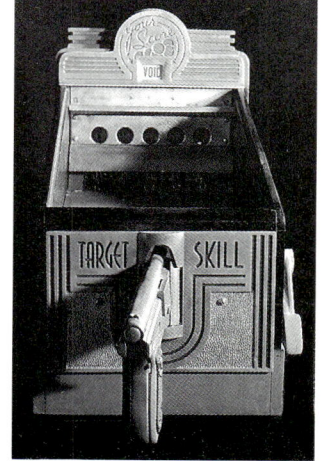

143

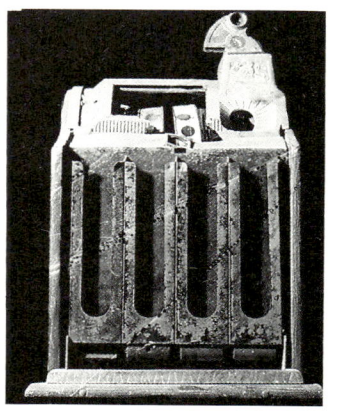

A	B	C	D
E	F	G	

144

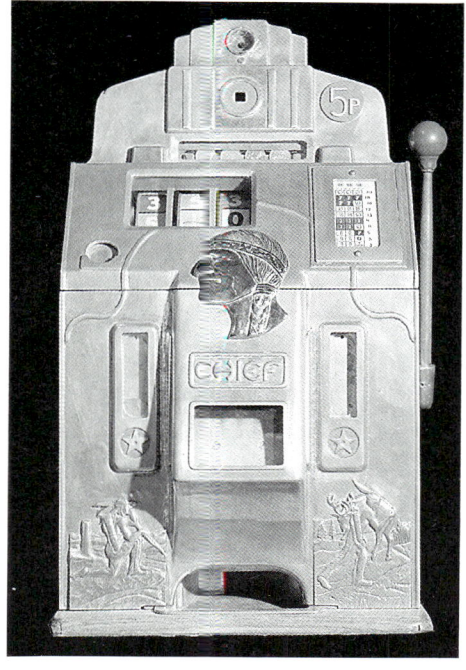
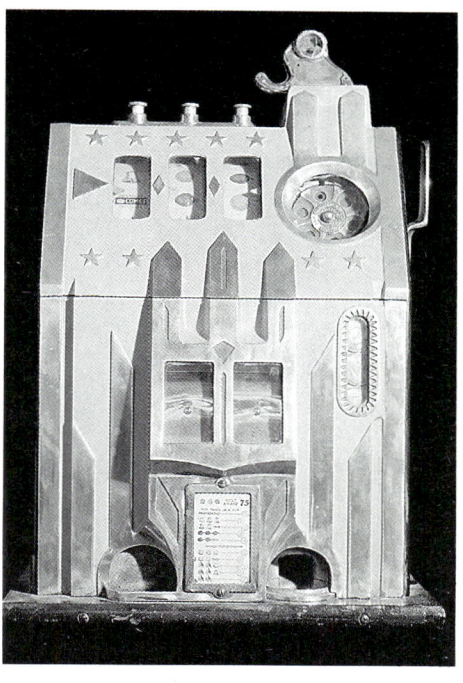

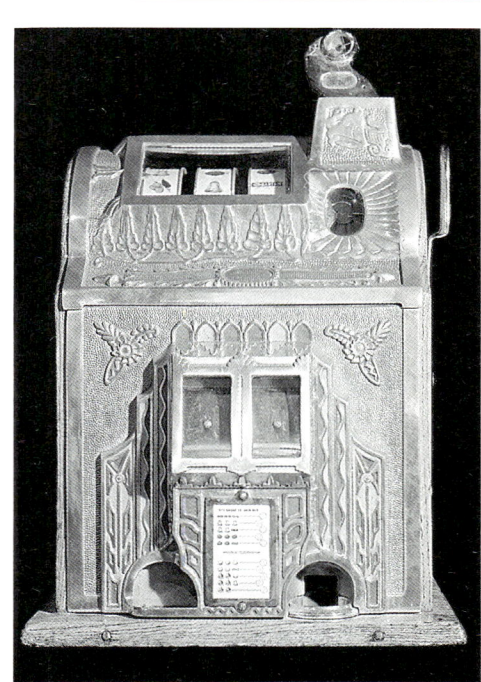

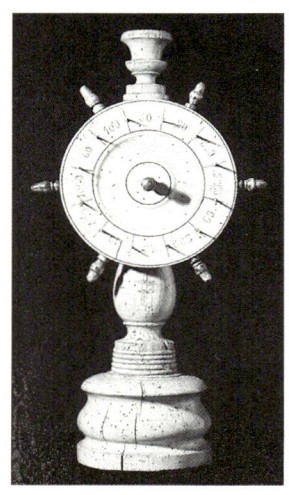

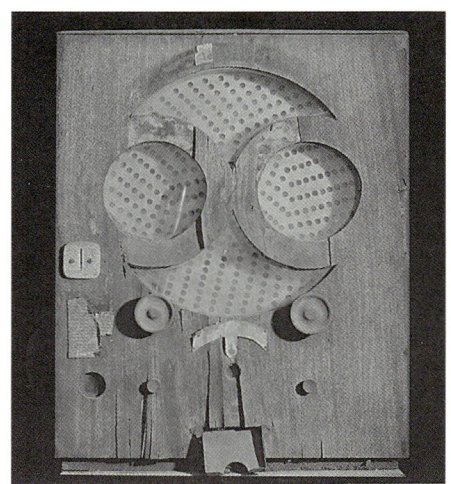

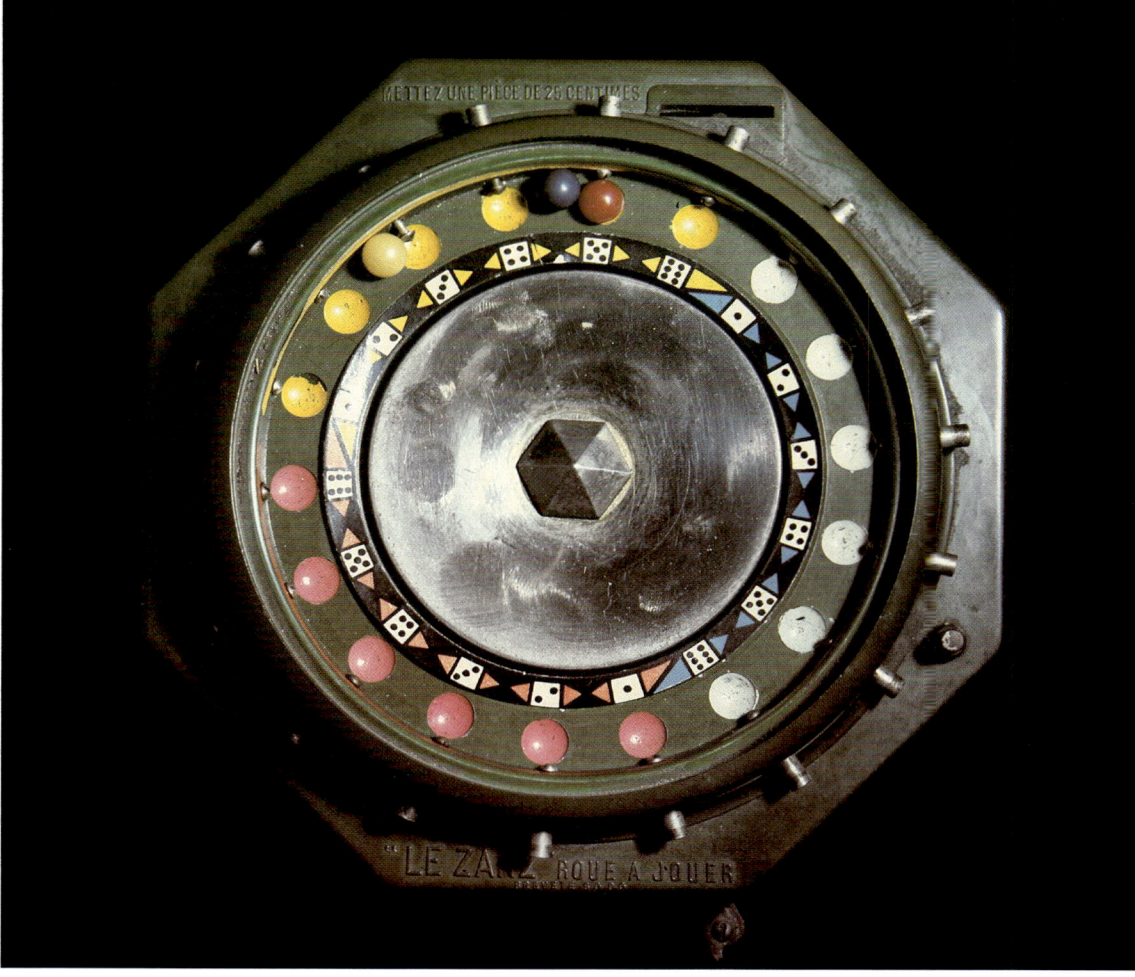

A	B
C	D
	E

A B
C D E

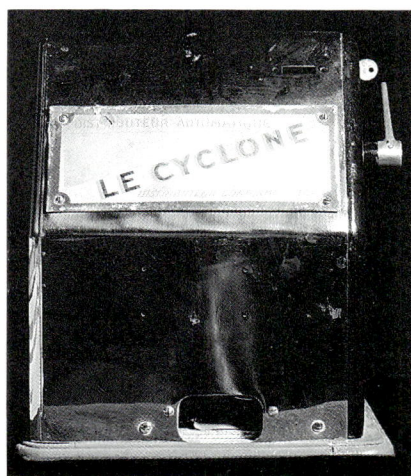

A B
C D E

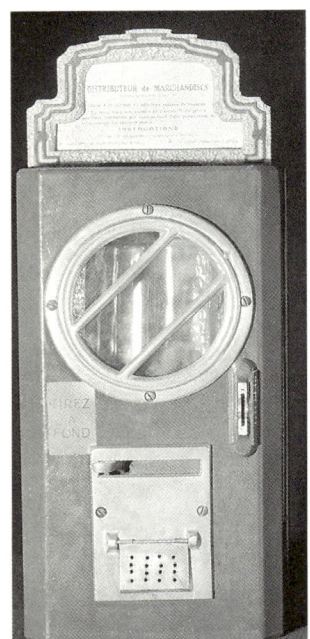

150

151

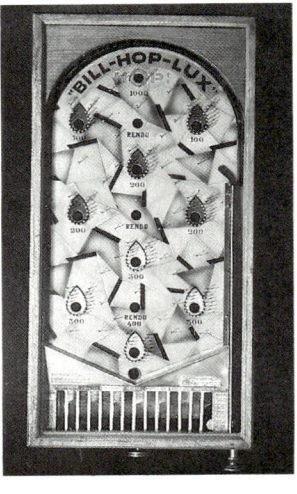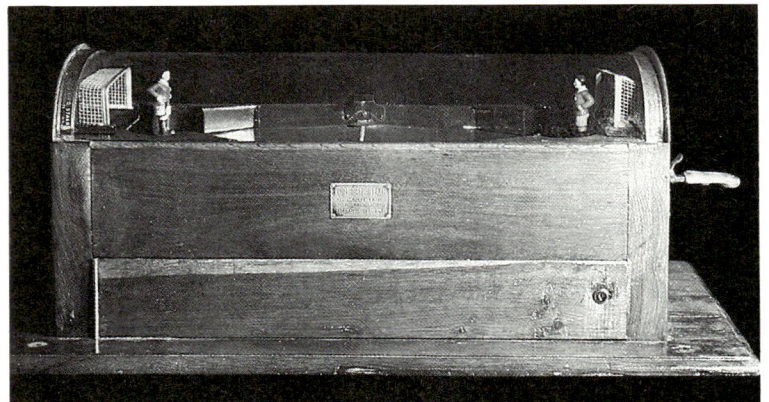

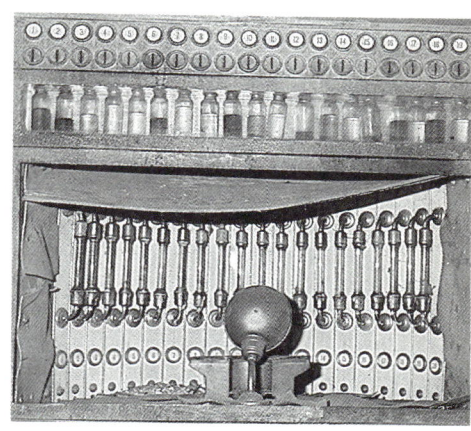

A	B	C
D	E	

11

12

Identification and Sources of Information

Identifying a coin-operated machine involves finding its name, the manufacturer's name and the date of invention, all of which is a kind of gamble in itself. Like pictures, some machines are signed with initials alone or not signed at all, some are undated and sometimes the subject is not even clear. But at least with paintings there are plenty of reference sources, specialists and experts. For slot machines however, sources of information are rare, details are often unlisted or, even worse, contradictory.

Faced by the overwhelming enthusiasm of players at the beginning of the century most makers pretended, for the publicity and prestige, that they were the first to have invented this or that machine. They circulated a great deal of misleading information and happily antedated their creations. For example there is the case of Charles Fey, the inventor of the first 3 reel automatic pay out machine. He ascribed the year of its invention at various times as 1887, 1889 or 1895, although no independent evidence of its existence remains prior to 1905/6. Further research is difficult since his workshop and archives were destroyed during the great fire of San Francisco.

Enquiries, long shots and unconfirmed evidence are not always enough, so several machines remain hopelessly anonymous while others could well be disputed in the future. To identify machines in this catalogue, I have used published documentary sources and my own unpublished archives, notably those of the two main French importers of American machines before the 1914 war, Cleophas Tricart of Rosult-Saint-Armand near Valenciennes and Victor Germain of Nantes, importers for Caille Brothers and Mills Novelty Company respectively. I questioned former owners and direct descendants of other manufacturers (Madame Martin, Adrien Mays' grand-daughter, Pierre-Louis and Pierre-Maurice Nau, Simone Bussoz, Raymond le Dentu, Marshall and Franck Fey, David A Mills etc.) I am also indebted to the work of Nicholas Costa whose research and efforts have helped to set the history of automatic machines on a firmer footing.

13

11/12/13 Matador / Wa-Wo-Na / Oracle. Contemporary sales literature identifies the manufacturers of the slot machines numbered 42, 93 and 3.

14

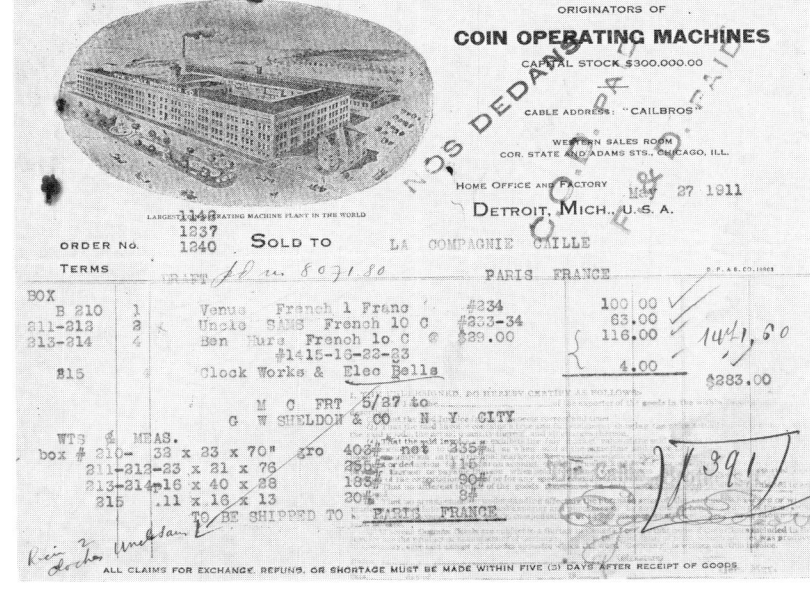

15

14. An amusing advertisement for William Klumpke, who contrary to all appearances just sold under his own name, machines imported by him from the USA, in this case the Owl by Mills.

15. A consignment note to Caille Brothers, Paris dated May 27th, 1911, itemising one Venus, two Uncle Sams, four Ben-Hurs and spare parts.

16. A fragment of literature concerning a machine built by Bignell about 1900.

17. A letter heading from Abel Nau.

18. Exhibition medals won by A. Mays.

16

French Manufacturers of Automatic Machines

17

18

A M P
Automatic cinemas (exhibition May 1935)

ANGELIQUE A Juvisy-sur-Orge
Known from an advertising card for the POLO wall machine circa 1905 describing himself as a manufacturer, designer and operator of coin operated machines.

APPAREILS CONTROLEURS (les)
"Ersic" coin freed lighter fluid dispensers - exhibited by May in 1935.

AURIEZ
Advertised a large machine known as Le Pilon (The Stamper) in December 1936.

AUTOMATIC S A M P Juvisy-sur-Orge
Advertised a coin freed roulette game February 1935.

AUTOREFLEX Paris
Made l'Autoroute Sportive. The first version was made in 1934, the second in 1935. Invented by Monsieur Billon, the founder of the firm.

AVION BOMBARDIER (L') Paris
Avion Bombardier (The Bomber) advertised in September 1935.

BARLAN
Mentioned in 1961 by Louis Loubet as a forgotten pioneer of automatic machines.

BARME Paris
The company was founded in 1899. Produced Mephisto roulette game; l'Athlete Complete (a strength tester); l'Oiseau Siffleur (Whistling Bird); a series of Fortune Tellers : Miss Tyka, Cartomancienne, Margeurite, Oracle de Satan; Fortune Card Dispensers and Electric Shock Machines. Exhibited June 1935.

BERAUD
A manufacturer flourishing in the first quarter of the 20th century. His wall machines included 5 Gagnants, le Taxi, le Magic, le Diabolic. Also the roulette la Merveilleuse which was identical to the model marketed by Bussoz.

BIGNELL E C Paris
Manufacturer, operator and distributor of coin freed machines 1903 - 1930s, he marketed upwards of 100 different machines. Wall machines : le Triomphe. Roulettes : IMO, Modern Roulette and le Bicyclette with 2 dials. 3 Reelmachines : le Juge de Paix, known in the UK as the Domino. During the 1930s he gave up manufacturing and became the French distributor for O D Jennings & Co of Chicago. He invented the Little Duke which he patented and was later manufactured under licence by Jennings.

BLAIVE
Invented la Roulette Divinatrice and applied for a patent in July 1935.

BLANC
Mentioned by Louis Loubet in 1961 as a forgotten pioneer of automatic machines.

BLANCHARD L
The Fortuna and the Rolling Poker were advertised by him in April 1935.

BONZINI et SOPRANSI Bagnolet
This company was founded in 1924 as Sopransi and Bonzini. They made an automatic phonograph in 1931 which was distributed by Bussoz. Roulettes (1932) : la Boule, le Vel d'Hiv, le Montlhery, le Pingouin. Pintables (1934) : l'Aero Golf, le Tour de Paris. Cranes (1935-37) : Grue SB, SB, Rotary Merchandiser (under licence to Exhibit Supply Co USA).

BOSI Aubervilles
Electric Cranes. 1930s.

BOUDOT G Pre Saint-Gervais
Cranes : le Pont Neuf (1935), le Couple (1936), la Vraie de Vraie (1936), la Joute (1936), Telesco Merchandiser (1937). Counter game : Tit Tat Tot.

BRAESCH A Paris
Turn of the century manufacturer of electric shock machines, strength testers, roulettes etc.

BUSSOZ Paris
Pierre Bussoz (1872-1958) is one of the most important French manufacturers of coin freed machines : wall machines, fortune tellers and roulettes such as Roulette Bussoz, la Belote, la B...Z, la Merveilleuse. 3 reel games : Paris Courses,

Roulettes Visible. Juke Boxes : Bussophone.

CASTILLE et HADENBACK Enghien les Bains Strength testers. 1935.

CHALLIER
General secretary of the Syndicat des Distributeurs de Confiserie - a euphemism for the operation of 3 reelers. Exhibited May 1935.

CHAPSAL B
A manufacturer of coin freed devices at the turn of the century. Louis Loubet was apprenticed to him when he was 13 years old in 1908.

CINEMATIC
Automatic cinematographs. Exhibited May 1935.

COLOMBO
Exhibited May 1937.

CONCORDIA
Made le Veinal fisherman crane. Exhibited May 1935.

CONORE Paris
Distributor of coin freed postage stamp machines. Patent granted in 1899.

CONSTANTIN
Crane, le Pelleur, invented by Maurice Arnouil in 1935.

COURSON Neuilly
Wall machine : Joker Boul in 1936.

COUSIN Lille
Exhibited May 1936. Russian billiards, French billiards, advertising signs. Horse racing games : la Sautrelle, le Plus Malin, l'Enigme. Football games : le Petit Football Kientz Cousin. Bowling game : le Federal Cousin. Roulette game.

DEROUIN Paris
Advertised as a manufacturer but was essentially a distributor and importer, most notably of machines made by Tura in Leipzig.

D I
Le Sphinx

DWEK Paris
Automatic machines exhibited by May in 1936.

ETIENNE
Exhibited in May 1937.

FEBA
Automatic machines exhibited in May 1936.

FLEURY Paris
Le Quick 1936.

FORESTY
Firm founded by Louis Miquel, inventor of the Jockey, the Bol d'Or and the Chasse a Courre. 1934-36.

FORTUNIO
The Princess was the only French 3 reeler made in the style of US one arm bandits. It was exhibited by May in 1937 along with another of the company's products, the Tierce et Belote.

GEHAM & CO Paris
Automatic machines exhibited in May 1936.

GERMAIN V Nantes
Founded in 1906 as a coin machine manufacturing company. They were important operators in Brittany.

GOUBY R
Cranes : RG5 (1935) and la Peche Magnetique (1935).

GRASSET I Marseilles
Trade stimulator : l'Etonnant 1898.

GRAVELAIS
Roulettes exhibited May 1935.

GUILLEBERT Jargeau (Loiret)
A manufacturer briefly in partnership with Raymond le Dentu.

HELAIN
Crane : les Baguettes Chinoises. Exhibited May 1937.

HOLDING AUTOMATIC
Roulettes : Derby, PMU, Poker. Exhibited May 1937.

HUGUENIN
Cranes.

JADAP Paris
Vending machines. Exhibited May 1936.

J A F (les Jouets et Automates Francais). Paris
Founded 1865. Made le Pecheur (1934), l'Accordeon Jazz, l'Oiseau Chanteur, le Pere Magloire and dozens of other automatons.

J A K Paris
A company owned by Kermesse Berlitz during the 1930s : Jack Hockey (1935), Le Phare (6 Sided Crane 1935), Skee Ball Jako. Advertised in October 1937.

JORAY Vaux-Andigny
Zanzi, Poker, Roue d'Argent. Advertised in May 1936.

KIENTZ Lille
Exhbited le Petit Football in 1937 with Cousin - see reference under Cousin also.

KIK
Cranes : le Selectif. Advertised October 1936.

LAMAZIERE
Manufacturer in early 20th century mentioned by Loubet.

LA PRECISION
Distributors of a wide variety of vending machines designed for use in theatres, railway carriages and outdoor locations. Exhibited May 1935.

LE COSAQUE Paris
Cigarette lighter fuel dispensers.

LE DENTU R Orleans (1881-1947)
A very important French manufacturer. Made wall machines : le Dedale, le Rafale, l'Entraineur, l'Auto, le Tourbillon, la Chasse - a shooting game known in the UK as The Hare. Le Dentu was in partnership with Guillebert for a time.

LEGRIS
Exhibited May 1937.

LEONI Paris
One of the earliest French manufacturers of vending machines for sweetmeats, liquids and other articles. La Poule Pondeuse Automatic, circa 1897, was a postage stamp vender (patented 1899). Auto Clown (on polyphon, patented 1899). Photographic automaton (patented 1899). Vending machine in the shape of a rabbit (patented 1899).

LEROUX R G
Crane : le Tour de France 1937.

LOUBET L (1895-1979) La Garenne-Colombes
French manufacturer who claimed to have made his first machine in 1910. He was president of the trade society following the death of Bonzini in 1937. Shooter : l'Eclair. Roulette : Poker d'As. New Shooter (advertised in 1935). Roulette : la Comte 1936, TSF 1958. Made the first model of a parking meter, the Taxiparc, to be used at Orly Airport in 1960.

LUDO
A company formed by Gastaud and Raibaut. Wall mounted vender : Stella, advertised in 1935. Les Boxeurs, Starway pingame, le Tir aux Pigeons (1935, invented by Crettien).

MABILLE
Coin operated scales.

MALCUIT C
Le Distributor, la Roulette CM (advertised October 1936), l'Hippodrome, le Steeple (advertised June 1937), le Globe.

MARCHANT Levallois
Crane : EMA 1937.

MARTIN & CO Amiens
Electric Flags, Rosette, automatic cinematograph, Football Staar (invented by the Belgian, Staar).

MARTINACHE
La Tierce et Belote, the first French 3 reeler made in the style of American machines.

MAYS A (1863-1923) Paris
Without doubt one of the earliest French manufacturers. He invented among other things a machine for making safety pins for which he was awarded a gold medal in

Amsterdam in 1883. One of the earliest makers of roulette games.

M B
Course de Levriers (a large pingame) advertised March 1937.

M E (Mondiale Exploitation)
Crane : Normandie Lumineuse, advertised february 1937.

MEYER
Electric shock machine

MICHELET M
Roulettes : M M, Outsider Olympic, Tricolor.

MICO
Kec-bell, a type of console, advertised July 1937.

MIQUEL
Founder of the Societe Foresty, inventor of the Jockey, Bol d'Or and the Chasse a Courre.

MULLER
Exhibited May 1937.

NAU A (1858-1936) Paris
Turn of the century importer of machines made by Clawson & Co in the US. He began making his own machines based on Clawson originals : Le Phenix roulette made with or without a musical box, countertop or freestanding versions, la Roulette Nouvelle. Le Coq Phenix wall machine in a number of different versions, les Petits Chevaux, les Trois Couleurs, la Petite.

NOVA. Lille
Automatic shooting game : le Tir Nova, a freestanding prize distributor, exhibited in May 1935. Nova introduced Russian billiards to France in July 1932.

O F A Paris
Crane : le Touring.

OMEGA Paris
Concours Hippique and Auto Ecole, advertised December 1937.

OTOMATO Paris
Domino Ticket, exhibited May 1936.

PASTEUR
Early French manufacturer of automatic machines. Wall machine : les Guguss, early 1900s.

PIERRE
Turn of the century manufacturer. Wall machines : le Turf, le Dirigeable, etc.

RAYMOND
Automatic machines exhibited May 1936.

ROPA (Societe) Neuilly
Automatic machines.

SARREAU A
Manufacturer and operator of automatic machines.

SCOTT-ADICKES & CO London
One of the largest importers of American made machines in France during the 1930s, most notably pintables.

S E M I S
Le Mistral, operated with compressed air. Advertised March 1937.

SERU G Paris
De luxe roulettes in walnut cases. Exhibited May 1937.

S E T A C Lyon
TSF automatic machines. Exhibited May 1936.

SINED
Two small countertop shooting games : Ali Baba and Beau Site. Exhibited may 1935.

S O M U E
Crane : le Pont Circulaire, 1937.

SPANAGEL H
Early 20th century manufacturer of wall machines : le Mexicain etc.

STEENBAKKERS F
Roulettes. Exhibited May 1935.

TAXIBRIQUET Paris
Small lighter fuel vending machine.

THOMMERET R Saint-Maur
Crane advertised a roulette game in April 1935 which allowed the player to score points, make words or hand of cards : the Magic Finger. Exhibited May 1935.

TOLERIE DE BOULOGNE Boulogne
Counter games with coloured balls : Tol Bol, le Cameleon, le Six Couleurs.

UNIC STELLA
Punchboards : Planchette Unic. Roulettes : le Tierce, la Roulette, le Quick. Exhibited May 1935.

Bibliography

Unpublished Archives

Adrien MAYS, 62 rue Marcadet, Paris 18 (1863 - 1923)
Diplomas, medals, correspondence.

CAILLE BROTHERS CO Paris agency: 12 rue de la Chaussee d'Antim.
Commercial correspondence (1910-11) advertisements, archives, Paris agency catalogues.

Cleophes TRICART, Rosult-St-Armand (Nord) (1868 - 1929) Mechanical piano manufacturer and importer for Caille Brothers: correspondence, accounts books, archives, catalogues.

Raymond LEDENTU, Orleans (1888 - 1947) Archives

Victor GERMAIN, Nantes, (Company established 1906) importer for Mills Novelty Co.
Archives and correspondence. Archives available for study at J-C Baudot, 7 rue Greffulhe, 75008 Paris.

Pierre Abel NAU, Paris (1858 - 1936) Nau family archives.

Pierre BUSSOZ, Paris (1872 - 1958) Bussoz family archives.

Old Manufacturers' and Agents' Catalogues

Instructions for Owl, Judge and On The Square machines by Mills, October 2nd 1904, 8pp.

Catalogue of coin operated Mills slot machines, circa 1905, 24pp.

Mills automatic machines. Export Catalogue. 1907. 48pp.

Mills automatic money makers. 1909

Mills coin operated machines. (How fortunes are made). Feb 1908. 100pp.

Mills automatic novelties (gum vendors, trade stimulators, amusement, athletic machines etc). 1913. 40pp.

Mills, coin operated slot machines in relation to G.N.P., 1938, 46pp.

Watling Manufacturing Co Special list of current prices, circa 1907. 10pp.

La Compagnia Caille, American made machines of every sort, leaflet 1910, 6pp.

Caille Amusement machines. Catalogue, 512, 1912 (?) 16pp.

Caille's Spanish catalogue, circa 1906, 94pp.

Cigar lighters that never fail, Eldred Manufacturing Co., Chicago, leaflet circa 1900, 12pp.

William Klumpke American automatic vending machines, circa 1903.

Abel Nau leaflets and advertisements, 1900-7.

Protti e Tonini. Slot machines and film cameras. Milan, April 1908, 32pp.

Rambo Society Price-list. June 15th 1933.

Sceniscope Co., The World in Motion. (The sceniscope), circa 1900. 36pp.

Bolland's Amusement Machine Supply Co. Ltd. Automatic amusement machines, ,circa 1935. 16pp.

Bonzini and Sopransi automatic games and machines, April 1937. 24pp.

Leaflet for Omnium automatic. Marseille - Paris - Chicago. 1934. 8pp

Reprints (USA)

Kernan Manufacturing Company Catalogue of supplies for saloon, billiard

hall and club room use. 1901. 64pp.
Mills. Directions for Mills operators

Bell : Counter OK Mint Vender, Front OK Mint Vender March 12th 1929. 16pp.

Mills. A safe investment. 1906. 28pp.

Pace. Parts list and service manual. April 1937. 40pp.

Mills. The anatomy of vintage slot machine.

Mike Munves arcade supply catalogue, 1956.

Caille Catalogue, 311, 1911 (?)

Mills model code and general instruction and part numbers for the vest pocket Bell, 1949. 16pp.

Owner's pictorial guide for the care and understanding of the Mills Bell slot machine (for post 1931 machines). 164pp.

Catalogue of golden opportunities, coin operated machines by Walter B Chandler. 1913. 52pp.

Slots and Stuff (Jennings advertisements compiled by Dave Evans). 1930's. 30pp.

Publications

Q D Bowers. *Encyclopedia of Automatic Musical Instruments. 1972.* 1,008pp. Black and white illustrations. The Vestal Press, USA.

D G Christensen. *Slot Machines, a Pictorial Review.* 1972. Revised reprint 1976. 123pp. Black and white illustrations. The Vestal Press, USA.

N Costa. *Articles 1981-88 in Worlds Fair, Coin Slot, Location, Nudge etc.*

N Costa. *Automatic Pleasures, the History of the Coin machine.* 1988. 224pp. Black & white and colour illustrations. Kevin Francis Publishing Ltd, London.

J-M Lhote. *Le Symbolisme des Jeux.* 1976. 356pp. Published by Berg International.

Les Jouers (Far West) 1978, French edition. 1980. 240pp. Illustrated. Time Life International.

K & F Rubin. *Drop Coin Here.* 1979. 96pp. Black/white and colour illustrations. Crown Publishers Inc, USA.

Slot Machines of Yesteryear series Mills of the Thirties. 192pp. Illustrated.
Mills of the Forties. 192pp. Illustrated.
Watling Operator's Companion. 192pp. Illustrated. Post Era Books, USA.

Collector's Treasure of Antique Slot Machines from Contemporary Advertising. 1981. 480pp. 700 illustrations. Post Era Books, USA.

Slot Machines on Parade. 1981. 224pp. Colour illustrations. The Mead Company, USA.

R M Bueschel. *Guide to the 100 Most Collectable Slot Machines.* Volume I. 1977. 118pp. Illustrated.
Volume II. 1979. 156pp. Illustrated.
Volume III. 1981. 142pp. Illustrated.
Volume IV. 1985. 150 pp. Illustrated. The Coin Slot, USA.

R M Bueschel. *Guide to the 100 Most Collectable Trade Stimulators.* 2 volumes. 1978-80. The Coin Slot, USA.

Alpert & Smith. *Amusement Tokens of the USA and Canada. 1979.* 148pp. The Mead Company, USA.

M Colmer. *The Great Vending Machine.* 1978. Contemporary Books Inc, USA.

R C Sharpe. *Pinball!* 1977. 192pp. Colour illustrations. Elsevier Publishing Company, USA.

J Krivine. *Juke Box on Saturday Night.* 1977. 160pp. Illustrated. New English Library, England.

M Colmer. *Pinball Machines,* French edition, 1976 124pp. Black/white and colour illustrations. Delville Publishers, France.

M Fey. *Slot Machines.* 1983. 240pp. Black & white and colour illustrations. Nevada Publications, USA.

B Enes. *Silent Salesmen.* 1988. 156pp. Black & white and colour illustrations. Enes Publishing, USA.

Periodicals

1. Past
Les Inventions Illustrees (1899)
La Revue de l'Automatique, monthly April 1934 (No.1) - December 1937
Numerous press cuttings from various sources.
Le Revue Mensuelle de l'Automatique (No.1, April 1960)

2. Present
L'Officiel de l'Automatique.
The Coin Slot, USA.
World's Fair, England.
Amusement Business, England.
Pinball Player and Penny Slot Collector, England.
Benelumat, Belgium.
Automat, Italy.
Munzautomat, West Germany.
Automatenmarkt, West Germany.
Pinball Collectors (quarterly)

Miscellaneous

Heron d'Alexandrie - *Pneumatica* (circa 200 BC)
Year 11 decree banning lotteries.

Index of Illustrated Machines

A

Ajax Puncher no 133, p 112
Answerite p 141, fig A
Apollo no 135, p 113
Athlete Complet no 132, p 111
Autophone p 151, fig D
Autoroute Sportive p 151, fig D
Avenir p 149, fig E
Avions no 34, p 47

B

Balances p 142, fig A,E;p 146, fig D
Balance de Gare no 129, p 109
Ball Gum Vender no 152, p 126
Bar Automatique p 153, fig E
Base-Ball Bell no 97, p 87
Belote Monaco no.68, p 69
Bijoux Pickwick no 15, p 36
Bill Hop Lux p 152, fig B
Billiard Vertical p 148, fig B
Black Beauty Bell no 109, p 95
Black Cherry Bell no 110, p 95
Blue War Eagle no 104, p 92
Bones no 45, p 54
Bonus Bell no 108, p 94
Boop a Doop no 122, p 104
Boule d'Or p 143, fig D
Bouteille no 76, p 73
Boxeurs no 126, p 107
Boxomat no 33, p 47
Bull Dog no 21, p 39
Bussophone 1920, no 163, p 136

C

Cagnotte, p 140, fig A
Caisse Enregistreuse p 153, fig D
Cameleon no 125, p 106
Carlo no 47, p 56
Cascade p 140, fig B
Ce que Disent Vos Yeux no 146, p 122
Chasse no 82, p 77
Chasse a Courre no 83, p 77
Chief Bell p 145, fig A
Chien Savant no 57, p 61
Clown no 19, p 38
Cochon Electriseur no 139, p 117
Comet Bell p 144, fig E
Comet no 26, p 43
Comet p 153, fig C
Commercial no 36, p 49
Confection no 102, p 90
Coq Phenix no 11, p 34
Cricket no 48, p 57
Cyclone p 149, fig D
Cyclone no 151, p 126

D

Deliver the Punch p 142, fig C
Derby no 71, p 71
Dicette no 115, p 99
Dirigeable no 142, p 119
Distributeur a Trous p 146, fig B
Domino no 94, p 85
Dominos n 100, p 89
Double p 139, fig D
Dough Boy Bell no 103, p 91
Douze<12> no 8, p 32
Duchess Bell no 107, p 93
Dutch Boy no 95, p 86

E

Eclair no 77, p 75
Ecureuil no 18, p 38
Egyptien no 143, p 121
Electra no 80, p 76
Electra no 81, p 76
Electriseur Barme p 150, fig E
Electriseur Vert p 141, fig B
Electrovender Executive no 92, p
Elephant no 156, p 128
Elite no 53, p 59
Elk no 43, p 53
Energie p 149, fig B
Etonnant no 116, p 100

F

Fair Play Bell no 112, p 96
Fairest Wheel no 114, p 99
Feu no 137, p 116
Film Stars no 31, p 46
F O.K. Vender no 91 p 82
F O.K. Vender p 144, fig F
Force de la Main p 142, fig D
Football Staar p 152, fig D
Footballeurs no 12, p 35
Francaise p 138, fig C
Freds p 150, fig F

G

Gauloise no 66, p 68
Globe no 40, p 51
Grand Prize Bell no 98, p 88
Grenouillere no 28, p 44
Grey Front Bell p 145, fig D
Guguss no 10, p 33

H

Haras no 32, p 46
Harvard Stamper p 153, fig A

Horse Race no 38, p 50

I

Improved Pickwick no 17, p 37
Inedit p 139, fig A
Iris no 62, p 66

J

Jackpot no 56, p 61
Jockey no 41, p 51
John Bull no 149, p 125
Joker Boul p 140, fig D

L

Labyrinthe Rouge p 151, fig C
Le Notre no 61, p 65
Liberty Commercial no 30, p 45
Liga p 152, fig E
Lighter Fuel Vender no 157, p 129
Little Dream no 54, p 60
Little Duke no 106, p 93
Little Perfection no 121, p 103
Loterie Royale no 113, p 98
Loteries de Comptoir no 117, p 100;
no 118, p 101; p 144, fig A, B;
p 146, fig A
Lutin p 139, fig B

M

Magic no 23, p 40
Malabar p 138, fig A
Malaussena no 153, p 127
Marguerite p 142, fig F
Matador no 42, p 52
Matches no 160, p 131
Mayflower no 119, p 102
Mephisto no 74, p 72
Merveilleuse no 60, p 64
Meyer p 150, fig D
Mille no 14, p 36
Mille no 44, p 53
Miss Tyka no 145, p 122
Monte-Carlo no 35, p 48
Motocine no 140, p 118
Muscle Tester no 130, p 110, 111
Musical Floor Machine no 4, p 29
Musical Fortune Teller no 6, p 30
Musicienne no 67, p 68
Musicienne no 72, p 71

N

Nain p 140, fig E

Negro Ball no 123, p 104

O

Olympia Puncher p 142, fig B
Omega no.90, p 83
Oracle no 3, p 28
Oracle p 141, fig C
Orage no 138, p 116
Owl p 138, fig B, D

P

Pace Blanche Comet Ball p 144, fig E
Pace Orange Star Bell p 145, fig B
Pace's Races no 39, p 50
Parking Meter no 158, p 130
Parcours Automobile p 151, fig B
Paris Courses no 84, p 79
Passe-Partout no 37, p 49
Pecheur no 147, p 124
Pere Bidard no 29, p 44
Perfection no 2, p 28
Petit Meyer no 136, p 115
Petits Chevaux no 27, p 43
Phenix, no 7, p 30
Phenix no 55, p 60
Pierrot no 9, p 32
Players Please no. 159, p 131
Polo no 20, p 39
Porte-Bonheur no 22, p 40
Post Card Vender no 150, p 125
Post Office no 144, p 121
Poule Automatique no 148, p 124
Poule Pondeuse Automatique
no 155, p 128
Profit Sharing p 149, fig A
Puce no 50, p 58
Puck no 1, p 27

Q

Queen Top no 128, p 107

R

Railway p 152, fig C
Rapid no 78, p 75
Regular O.K. Mint Vender no 89, p 82
Regular O.K. Mint Vender Bell p 145, fig C
Reliable no 5, p 29
Rol-A-Top no 87, p 81
Rolling Poker no 46, p 54
Roll Out The Barrel no 86, p 80
Rotuor no 162, p 133
Rouge et Noire no 65, p 67

Roulette de la Brocanteuse d'Amour no 73, p 72
Roulette Bussoz no 58, p 63; no 70, p 70; p 143, fig A, B p 147, fig A, B, D, E
Roulette Mays no 59, p 63
Roulette Nouvelle no 63, p 66
Roulette Serpent no 75, p 111
Roulette Visible no 85, p 79

S

Saint Dunstan's Horoscope p 149, fig C
Samson Lifter no 131, p 111
Sankt Hubertus Schiess no 79, p 76
Saturne p 152, fig A
Select Roulette no 69, p 70
Select Roulette p 143, fig F
Silent War Eagle Bell no 105, p 92
Simonia no 96, p 87
Simplex p 141, fig E
Six Coleurs p 141, fig D
Skee Ball p 151, fig E
Skyscraper Bell no 101, p 90
Soleil no 52, p 59
Sourire no 24, p 42
Sphinx no 51, p 58
Stamps p 150, fig A
Stella p 146, fig C
Stereoscope no 141, p 118
Super Poker no 120, p 103
Sweepstakes p 148, fig B

T

Target Skill p 143, fig E
Taxi no 13, p 35
Taxibriquet p 153, fig B
Tickette no 127, p 107
Tierce et Belote no 88, p 81
Tiger no 25, p 42
Tir Electra nos. 80 et 81, p 76
Tir Fritz p 143, fig C
Tol Boul no 124, p 105
Tonneaux no 16, p 37
Totalisator Bell no 111, p 96
Tour de Paris no 161, p 133
Triplette no 64, p .67
Trois Tetes p 147, fig C
Tura Bell no 99, p 88

U

Uncle Sam no 134, p 113
Unic no 49, p 57
Unic p 140, fig C

V

Vapolux no 154, p 127
Victoria Jackpot p 144, fig D
Victoria Peacocks Bell p 144, fig C

W

Wa-Wo-Na no 93, p 84
Wa-Wo-Na p 144, fig G
Win Easy p 148, fig C

Z

Zanz p 146, fig E